WHAT WILL MAKE YOU HAPPY?

THE COMPLETE GUIDE TO OVERCOME NEGATIVE THINKING AND FIND HAPPINESS IN YOURSELF

ROMA SHARMA

FIRST EDITION, SELF-PUBLISHED BY ROMA SHARMA
PRINTED IN INDIA

ISBN 978-93-5473-805-0

DISCLAIMER

This book is for informational purposes only. The views expressed are those of the author alone and should be implemented by the reader at his/her own responsibility. The information provided is of a general nature only.

WHY BE HAPPY?

We all want to be happy. We might not state it explicitly, but we hope for it. We live from one moment to another, unconsciously taking decisions based on what we believe will bring us happiness. Since most of our thinking happens on auto-pilot it might not be evident to us that we are constantly pursuing what we believe will be pleasurable and avoiding things that could cause us pain.

Let's look at the benefits of being happy, besides the good feeling you experience inside your mind and body. As a happy person, you make great company. You radiate charisma through your positivity wherever you go. People like being around you because you are easy to get along with. You attract the right people into your life by getting into the right state yourself.

When you are happy, you make good decisions and generate significant results. You are able to have great relationships too. Due to these factors, your self-esteem goes up. You are not afraid to try out new things. Opportunities follow you wherever you go. The belief that you can create the life you want can fill you with unshakeable confidence. You are likely to attract the things you desire because you thought it was possible. You don't feel insecure or envious of people who have achieved more. You are happy for them because, internally, you are happy for yourself too.

With an improved mood, your overall health improves. You are energized, motivated, and look forward to your day. All aspects of your life are interconnected. A gradual improvement in one has a domino effect on others. (*Domino effect* is when one event sets off a chain of similar events, creating a cumulative effect.)

INTRODUCTION

Your happiness is important to you. Your actions are unconsciously guided by your intention to promote your happiness. When you feel lonely you call a friend, eat comfort food, or listen to your favorite music. You do these things to feel better in the moment, and they work for you. However, sometimes these attempts backfire. For instance, you might call a friend and instead of feeling better, you might end up feeling worse; your food might not be as per your expectation and your favorite music might not comfort you either. You want to be happy, but your repeated attempts to achieve happiness leave you frustrated.

Wanting happiness and trying hard to get it causes desperation. It is like holding a fist full of sand. The tighter you grip it, the faster it slips away. The starting point is to find things that are going well for us and feel happy about them right now. If the internal strategy to create a feeling isn't there, it is hard to scale it by having *more* of anything.

Little children feel happy at the smallest of things, but it is difficult to get an adult to feel the same excitement. We are unable to feel happy at a random train or plane passing by. It is not just about changing interests; it is the decreasing capacity to find happiness in the little things in life.

Studies have shown that when people win a lottery, they feel happy for a while because of their sudden financial spike. However, this happiness is short-lived. Their emotional gravity pulls them back to their old state once the excitement wears off. This is known as the *Hedonic Treadmill*. Even if people experience tremendous loss and are overwhelmed with pain, their state lasts only so long. Extreme happiness or sorrow has a shelf-life, after which people return to their habitual state of mind—one that is familiar to them.

We might feel excited about a new project, work hard on achieving our goals, and feel the euphoria of success for a while. Soon this will become the new normal and we will become bored. The same project might not excite us as it had previously. The thrill of achieving our goals wears off, and we return to our baseline mood.

This is how we feel most of the time. We are back to wanting more; something or someone to bring those good feelings back—that next increment, promotion, or partner that we believe will make us happy. This time we need to peddle harder, as the next experience needs to measure up to the last one.

If we have indulged in eating, drinking, or any substance to feel better, we will also have to deal with the aftereffects of it. When our mind is stressed, our body pays the price. Stress by itself is enough to damage the body, with or without the use of *pick-me-ups*. An unconscious craving for happiness keeps us running after things. The excitement of our achievements is fleeting while the quest for happiness seems eternal.

> *All striving is after a fantasy*
>
> *- Fritz Perls, Psychiatrist & Founder of Gestalt Therapy*

Happiness seems like a *thing* we want but is actually a *state;* more like an adverb than a noun. We don't *have* happiness; we *do* things happily. We are not looking for a beautiful ship that we can own, rather, one that will help us sail through life smoothly.

Our Focus

The focus of this book is on what you can do to create your happiness rather than how people and situations could be. You didn't choose the cards life gave you, but you can play your hand well.

We might want people to be kinder to us, more understanding of our problems, or supportive of our endeav-
ors. However, we might not always have the conditions
we are looking for. We might have had an option while
choosing our jobs or partners, but we didn't choose our
families. There are people and situations in our life that
can't be changed. When those become our trouble-
zones we end up feeling helpless. We need to discover
new ways of thinking that can help us be happy, despite
unconducive external conditions.

Let's deep dive into the happiness pool and unravel
what exists there—something important to us, yet it
remains elusive. What is it we need to feel happy and
how can we make it last? How much of it comes from
our external environment and how much of it comes
from within? Can we create a space in our mind where
we can cultivate a garden of peace and happiness—a
place where we can stroll whenever we want and
possibly even live? I am glad to tell you that we can do
all this and much more by making a few simple
changes to our thinking patterns.

In this book you will discover:

- The principle factors that determine your
  happiness
- A comprehensive list of distortions in thinking
- Effective ways to overcome negativity and
  stress

- Steps to improve your self-esteem and strengthen your relationships
- How to deal with bad memories and resentment
- How to find your life's purpose and align with it

Having worked as a coach for seven years at the time of this writing, I have had the opportunity to work with people who were struggling with their life situations and didn't believe they could be happy again. It has been a privilege to see them successfully turn their lives around. I have detailed the methods that worked for them in this book. These methods will work just as well for you, if implemented correctly.

I am confident that you can overcome any thoughts that are holding you back from being happy. Even if you have tried many things before that might not have given you the desired results, you are very likely to discover some methods that could transform your life today. The fact that you are reading this book indicates you are ready to make that change.

Do you also want to discover the 7 best ways to be yourself confidently and unapologetically? In the book, **What Will People Think?** you will find a complete guide to stop caring about what others think.

Also By
Roma

Log onto romasharma.com to discover the full
series.

What readers say about **What Will People Think?**:

"This book has all the elements one needs to succeed
without getting influenced by people's opinions"
"This book helped me get rid of my limiting beliefs"
"A simple, easy read with lots of examples I can
relate to"

Log onto romasharma.com and buy your copy of
What Will People Think? today!

DOWNLOAD YOUR FREE 'BEING YOURSELF JOURNAL'

Subscribe to my newsletter and receive a FREE copy of the Being Yourself Journal with powerful self-coaching questions. Log onto romasharma.com

Your FREE Book!

For more books log onto
romasharma.com

Here is what you will find in the journal:

1. Page templates that you can fill out every day to connect with your thoughts and feelings

2. Affirmations to increase self-esteem and confidence
3. Self-coaching questions that will help you find solutions in difficult situations
4. Simple ways to decrease worry and stay calm in the present moment

Download now! Log onto romasharma.com

4

———

HOW TO USE THIS BOOK

Please download the free **Being Yourself Journal** provided with this book by logging onto romasharma.com and referring to the self-coaching questions before you get started.

While reading the book, **What Will Make You Happy?** mark the sections which you believe you need to address. On completing the book, it is recommended that you revisit those sections and do the associated exercises. After that, please do the exercises in the other sections as well. You are likely to make some important discoveries that could transform your life.

Read your answers again after a few days. Each time you will interpret your thoughts differently based on the mood in which you read them, resulting in fresh takeaways.

Please note:

1. The words *subconscious* and *unconscious* are used interchangeably in this book.

2. *Un-resourceful states* or *negative emotions* refer to emotions that might make us uncomfortable, such as anger, hurt, guilt, or disappointment. The term *negative emotion* is used for ease of understanding and not to denote that these emotions are bad for us. Even uncomfortable emotions are helpful as they tell us what doesn't work for us. This information helps us make better choices in the future.

3. A male or female gender might be used in certain contexts. That does not imply any particular problem or situation to be related specifically to that gender. Please assume gender neutrality while reading this book.

5

YOUR FEELINGS CREATE YOUR REALITY

What needs to happen for you to be happy? Try reversing the sequence—start with being happy and whatever you desire will come your way.

Let's say you were going to hire a person for a certain job. If you see that she lacks confidence in doing the job, would you still hire her? Probably not. If the candidate needs to have a job in order to feel confident, it might take a while. Instead, if she could be confident now, the chances of her getting the job will go up. *Being* confident comes before *having* the job. Not the other way around.

Similarly, if you want to find a partner to be happy, start with being happy. Your energy will attract the right partner into your life. If you want a partner first and then you believe you will be happy, it might take longer. That's the way it is for most things we want. Instead of chasing our objects of desire, if we master our state, whatever we want will find its way into our life.

I often hear advice such as-

You should focus on your work to create better results.

You should have better relationships to be happy.

These statements are true. However, they might not account for the fact that a *feeling* is required to achieve these things. If you aren't able to focus, there might be something that's bothering you. If you aren't able to maintain healthy relationships, there could be certain underlying beliefs resulting in that situation. It might be difficult for us to put our finger on it, since each of us has different life situations and thinking patterns. We don't have a *one-size-fits-all* solution. The only way to discover what will make us happy is to explore different aspects of our life and see which one qualifies best as an area of work. Do we need better relationships with people or with ourselves? Do we need improved health or a different purpose in life?

By the end of this book, I aim to detail all aspects that could stand between you and your happiness. You will get complete clarity on what you need to be happy.

Effect of Mood on Thoughts

Your mood impacts your thoughts and your behavior. Let's say your business just made a huge profit. You are singing a song and walking back home with a spring in your step. Suddenly, a car drives past and accidentally splashes muddy water on you. You might frown at the driver for a moment but will soon get back to humming your song because you can't get over your big news.

Now, let's say, your business made a loss and you can't find a way to recover from it. You are walking home in despair and a car splashes muddy water on you. Will you drop it and move on? Probably not. You might shout angrily at the driver and walk home gloomier than before.

When the stimulus was the same, what changed your response? It was your mood.

Mood-based Recall

Anna and Emily are good friends. However, sometimes Anna feels that Emily is selfish, maybe because of a few experiences that led her to believe so. She doesn't nurse grudges against Emily. She leaves her experiences in the past (or so she thinks).

One day, Anna finds out that Emily has bought a dress; one that Anna liked very much and wanted to buy. It was the last piece in a designer's signature collection. She is thrilled, assuming that Emily bought it to surprise her on her birthday.

On Anna's birthday, Emily wears that dress to her party, leaving her shocked and heartbroken. She can't believe why Emily would do something like that to her. Emily knew how keen Anna was on having that dress, but bought the last piece for herself anyway.

Anna couldn't enjoy her birthday party. She started remembering how Emily had treated her in 9th grade, when she went out with someone she knew Anna had liked. She recalled how in 10th grade, she didn't share her study notes. Her disappointment grew as she remembered other events that proved how selfish she was.

Does it mean Anna doesn't like Emily? Or does she feel that way only when something specific happens?

Anna's thought process is because of her *mood-based recall*.

When you experience this, based on your mood, you will recall events you experienced earlier that match your mood. So, if you are angry with someone, you are likely to remember the times when that person did other things that made you angry. If you don't have a history with that person, you might recall times when someone else made you feel that way.

Similarly, when you are in a good mood, because someone said or did something nice, you are likely to recall the times when you felt the same way. Let's say, your colleague appreciates you for being hardworking, and you feel happy about it. You might remember the times she told you something similar, or other people who said the same thing about you.

We are wired to recall events that match the feelings we are experiencing in a given moment. Stronger the feelings, sharper the recall.

A mood that arises from a powerful emotion is like a little life form. Once it's born, it tries to grow. It uses your mental map of events to chain all similar events so it can stay alive. This applies to negative events as well as positive ones. For instance, people are programmed to see good things in the ones they love. Even if their flaws are obvious to everyone else, for them, they don't exist.

There is a study that suggests that the recall for less intense feelings also matches and fetches its equivalent state from our memory. If you are studying for an exam in a certain state of mind, you can recall information better, if you match that state. For instance, if you study in a calm state of mind, you can recall better if you stay calm while writing the exam. Students can use this information to their advantage, and so can others when they need to remember something.

In Anna's case, she thinks of Emily as a friend and doesn't nurse any grudges. However, when she is gripped by an emotion of extreme disappointment, on seeing Emily wearing the dress she wanted, she remembers all the times Emily behaved selfishly. She doesn't routinely play those memories in her mind—only when something swings her back into *that* mood.

If you have ever tried pepping up a friend, you might have noticed that it is indeed difficult to change a person's feelings by asking her to do so. You might not understand why she is in despair and fails to remember the times she has succeeded. You can see what she can't because you both are in a different mood. You are remembering the times when you solved problems, while she is remembering the times when she couldn't. That's why saying things like, *forget it,* or *change your mood,* doesn't work. We will go over ways to change our feeling states later in the book.

Mood-based Interpretation

Your interpretation of events matches your mood. If you are calm, you might give others the benefit of the doubt. Let's say you are running a race and someone pushes you off-track, you could interpret it as an accident, but if you are in a bad mood, you might suspect sabotage. Similarly, if you are experiencing road rage, you could perceive a driver who is honking and trying to overtake you as aggressive. However, if you are relaxed, you might quickly make way, believing the person has an emergency.

Just like your recall, your interpretation of situations also matches your mood. It is another way your mood stays alive.

Children realize this early on. If they need permission for something, they read their parents' mood to decide which of them to approach. They are also aware that their parents reprimand them, not based on the gravity of their mistake, but on the intensity of their mood. The response of the parent varies based on his/her interpretation. When they are in a good mood they may think, *"It's okay, she is just a child,"* and when they aren't, they might interpret the child to be irresponsible.

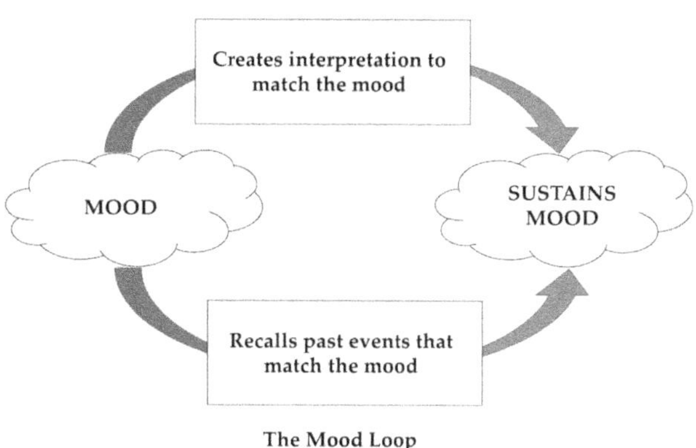

The Mood Loop

If you are in an un-resourceful state, you can break the loop from either direction to feel better—change your mood or your interpretation. We will go over ways to do this in the sections, Distortions in Thinking and Change Your Feeling.

6

AUTOMATIC NEGATIVE THOUGHTS: STRESS REACTION

Life is a mirror of your consistent thoughts

- Napoleon Hill, Author

Our thinking pattern largely decides our state of mind. Our mind creates approximately 60,000 thoughts a day. When we are stressed, these numbers go up significantly. Our thoughts become uncontrollable and don't follow any logical sequence. Thousands of them hit us automatically. Almost 80% of these thoughts are negative and hence are known as *Automatic Negative Thoughts.*

The following model is called the Cognitive Triad and was first proposed in 1976 by a Psychiatrist, Aaron Beck. Automatic Negative Thoughts are divided into three categories based on our core beliefs about ourselves, the world, and people. A disturbing event triggers a series of negative thoughts that could fall into one of these categories:

1) **The Self**: I am worthless. I don't like myself.

2) **The World**: Nobody cares about me. Everyone is against me because they know I am worthless.

3) **The Future**: Situations will always be bad. I'll never be good at anything.

Believing that the event we are experiencing is about us, generalizing it to reflect negatively on all areas of our life and believing things will always be the same, makes us experience despair. It clouds our mind and prevents us from seeing ways to turn our situation around.

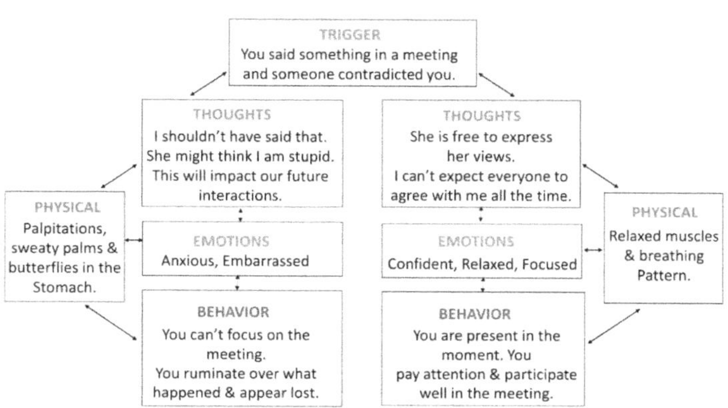

JIM'S MANAGER asked him to be the key note speaker at a Corporate Tech Summit. Jim is excited at the idea of representing his company, but public speaking scares him. His first reaction is-

Oh God, why did they pick me? Don't they remember how I goofed up last time?

Public speaking is just not my thing.

Who will want to listen to me?

As thousands of such thoughts race through his mind, he feels anxious. He experiences the anxiety physically in his body in the form of palpitations, sweaty palms, and chest pain. Post this emotional shift, he looks at things differently too. His thoughts become distorted and add to the negativity he was already experiencing. This cycle continues in a down-ward-spiral fashion, distorting his perception of reality.

The quality of Jim's thoughts reflects his deep-seated beliefs. In the sequence below, his beliefs have been written in **bold** and in parentheses against his corre-sponding thoughts-

Oh God, why did they pick me? Don't they remember how I goofed up last time? **(If I don't succeed once, I will never succeed)**

Public speaking is just not my thing. **(I am not good enough)**

Who will want to listen to me? **(People don't like me)**

A variety of thoughts could come up for him, but the underlying core belief is the same—I am not good enough. Even if people try to encourage him by reminding him of his accomplishments, he might not change his views until he changes his core beliefs about himself.

Why do we have Automatic Negative Thoughts?

The creation of negative thoughts in response to a stressful situation is an evolutionary trait designed to keep us safe. When we face negative situations, we store the experience in our body. Our brain develops neural pathways for that emotion which gets strengthened on repetition. This plays back as a memory when a similar situation arises in the future, generating an involuntary response helping us fight perceived danger, just like an animal that automatically feels anxious on seeing a predator and runs to protect its life. When similar reactions happen in human beings, over events that only *appear* to be life-threatening, it can be self-limiting—like the fear that prevents people from taking risks or being creative.

How to deal with Automatic Negative Thoughts?

The best way to deal with automatic negative thoughts is to observe them. Trying to control them, aggravates them. Resistance to your thought process results in having more to resist.

Whatever you resist, persists

- Carl Jung, Psychiatrist

Take a few moments to remove yourself from the stressful environment and calm down. Next, separate yourself from your thoughts and look at them as unique entities. This process is known as *metacognition*. It is about being aware of your thoughts and being able to analyze them, without being attached to them. It helps in catching unhelpful thinking styles that could take a toll on your mind, body, and relationships. We will see how to analyze thoughts from a neutral position in the section, Disassociation.

7

DISTORTIONS IN THINKING

Your unconscious programming—your beliefs, values, attitudes, memories, and decisions—drive your focus and interpretation. When you experience an event, it gets filtered based on these factors to create an internal representation that is unique to you. This is a distorted version of reality because it has gone through several layers of filtering. (For more details on this, please refer to the section, Internal Thinking Engine, in my book, Thinking Habits For Definite Success.)

As we go through life, we might not have the opportunity or the appetite to clarify our views with others. We don't really *know* the people we think we know. We make assumptions that fit well with *our* story and twist the incoming facts until they align with what we already believe to be true. It's just easier that way. We don't want to change our beliefs, as that would mean challenging ourselves, which is scary. Hence, we go about life with unchallenged distortions inside our mind.

Distortions are the lies we tell ourselves which feel like the truth to us.

We don't know if somebody likes us or not, but we believe we do; we don't know why somebody turned down our offer, but we have a reason for it. We tend to complete our stories inside our mind because questioning our thinking is unnatural to us.

When you are in an un-resourceful state, ask yourself-

How do you know what you are thinking is true?

Are there any underlying assumptions in your thoughts?

You cannot fully do away with your distortions, but you can minimize their impact by being aware of what they do to you. Recognize that you can't fully comprehend reality—why people are the way they are, what they think about you, why something didn't turn out the way you wanted it to. You are likely to assume things because it is impossible to know *everything* about *everyone.*

Acknowledging that your thoughts could be misrepresented facts is an important step in changing them.

Let's look at some common distortions we experience in our daily life, and how they can be addressed. While going over the list of distortions, contemplate which ones might be more applicable to you. All distortions in thinking don't need to be addressed. Based on how they affect your life, some might be useful to you. If a distortion helps you, retain it. For instance, if you believe people like you and that makes you happy, you don't need to change it.

All or Nothing

The All or Nothing distortion is also known as *Black and White Thinking*. Each one of us has an unconscious checklist by which we decide if something is right for us. It helps us set standards in our life. It becomes problematic when we want *everything* in our checklist to be ticked off in order to be happy. For instance, if you are running a race, there is no value in coming second. You have to come first or you have *failed*.

People with the All or Nothing distortion pressurize themselves by setting exceptionally high standards and deny themselves happiness until they have matched or exceeded them. Their distortion causes them to pass harsh judgments on themselves, on others, and on situations. It results in rigidity and unrealistic expectations. This kind of polarized thinking is prominent in people who have a *'my way or the highway'* attitude.

Reeta wants her husband, Sam, to come home early every day from work, take her out on weekends, and buy her gifts. Sam isn't able to come home early *every day,* although he does on most days. On weekends he likes to relax and doesn't feel like going out, although he does take her out once a fortnight.

Reeta isn't happy with his efforts because Sam isn't able to do *everything* she wants. One day she gets angry and shuts him out. She wants him to meet her complete checklist, that being the only way she feels cared for.

Belief: If I don't have everything, I have nothing.

Challenge: Reeta's thinking can be challenged for an **All or Nothing** distortion by asking her the following questions-

What has to happen for you to feel cared for?

Despite his personal struggles, if Sam does some of the things you desire, isn't that caring as well?

Are you aware of Sam's checklist? Are you able to do everything he needs to feel cared for?

On exploring this direction, Reeta might realize that Sam is doing the best he can. To feel better, her expectations need to be reworked.

Over-generalization

Over-generalization is about making sweeping statements based on a few experiences. It can be observed when people pick one event that happened in one context and extend it to all other contexts as if there is no exception to their experience. For instance, if you visit a country and perceive one or two people as rude, you might generalize your observation to create a new belief: **all** *people in this country are rude.*

When we over-generalize we end up feeling *stuck* because we paint our experiences with a broad brush, often wiping out any finer distinctions that could have led to more choices. Over-generalization can be spotted by the use of words such as always, every time, everyone, nobody, everybody, each one, or whenever.

Belief: If something happens once, it will happen always.

Suzy had an amazing relationship with her partner, Peter, for three years. They were ready to get married when suddenly something snapped. Peter broke up with her, as he was not ready to commit to their relationship. Suzy had been involved with two people previously who had broken up with her on similar grounds.

She became disheartened and decided to never enter a relationship again. She told her friends that she plans to stay single all her life since she is *never* going to find anyone anyway.

Challenge: Suzy's relationships might have ended a few times previously, but this is not an accurate indicator of what will happen in the future. Her distortion can be challenged by asking her-

*How do you know you will **never** find anyone?*

*You did meet three people, even if things didn't work out. So, you **are** meeting people, aren't you?*

In my coaching sessions, I usually challenge such a belief with, "Anyway, you have had the opportunity to meet *all* the people in this world and so you *know* you can't possibly like anyone again. You are right." This makes them smile.

When you generalize beyond what people are already doing they find it quite humorous. They might not notice their generalization until somebody does it more than them. (This is a helpful strategy if you are working as a coach. It is important to establish rapport with the client before doing this.)

I once met an author who sent out a copy of her manuscript to a few publishers hoping they would publish it. When each of them rejected it, she started believing that nobody would ever publish her work. This got me talking about the Harry Potter script that was rejected a dozen times before it was published. It makes an interesting piece of evidence that the opinion of a few people does not decide the future of a person. Generalizing critical opinions can create a self-limiting belief that could stop the person from trying again.

Generalizations are commonly seen in people who are depressed. They group their painful episodes to draw strong conclusions—like they had a terrible life, the world is a selfish place, or their problems will never go away—resulting in despair.

When the missing pieces of their experience are brought to the forefront, their beliefs are likely to change. When this happens, it helps them feel better instantly. For example, if Suzy is reminded of a person who was willing to commit to her but *she* refused to do so, it might make her realize that her generalization isn't fully substantiated. It's not that people are always leaving her. Sometimes, she makes these decisions too. Would she want the person she parted ways with to think that he would find no one again? Probably not.

Mental Filter

People remember things the way they choose to. Due to this they sometimes dwell on the negative aspect of their experiences, discarding everything else, just like a drop of ink that colors the entire beaker of water blue.

Belief: One negative aspect makes the whole situation negative.

Emily invited guests over for dinner. She worked hard to ensure that everything was perfect—the house, table setting, food, and music. When her guests arrived, they loved the ambiance of the place and complimented her for it. One guest, William, said that he liked the food, but the potatoes needed a bit more cooking. That apart, everything was great.

Emily was disappointed to hear his remark. After her guests left she told her husband, Mac, that the evening was ruined because William didn't enjoy the food. Mac was surprised to hear this. He tried to convince her that William liked the food overall; he just thought that the potatoes needed more cooking.

Mac tried to show Emily the bigger picture but she felt no different. She believed that William had said that he liked the food because he was just trying to be nice to her. He didn't enjoy the potatoes, nor anything else.

Emily's disappointment stems from focusing on one detail of the evening, namely the potatoes, rather than looking at the evening as a whole.

Challenge: Her thinking can be challenged by asking her the following questions-

Does the entire evening get ruined because of what one person thought?

How can you be sure that William complimented you on the food only to be nice to you?

What has to happen for you to believe the event you hosted was a success? Can you expect all those things to happen at once?

Emily has been dwelling on one remark which she perceived as negative. Even if William intended it as such, it doesn't reflect on how the evening was. Once this point is brought forth, she is likely to feel better about the situation.

Disqualifying the Positive

This distortion stems from disqualifying positive experiences as if they *don't count*. In the previous example, William said that he liked the food. However, when Mac brought it up with Emily, she dismissed it as William *being nice*. She couldn't take his remark of liking the food as seriously as the one on potatoes.

When people disqualify the positive, the proverbial half-full glass does not exist.

They maintain a negative belief despite strong contrary evidence. (This distortion is similar to the mental filter but is nonetheless distinct, because the mental filter is about focusing on the negative aspect of a situation; the positive aspect may or may not be discounted.)

Belief: The positive experiences don't count. I got them by luck, fluke, or other conditions that happened to be in my favor.

Challenge: Emily's thinking can be challenged by asking her-

Did your guests say anything positive about the evening? Did you spend as much time thinking about those comments?

People who disqualify the positive often reject compliments. Let's say a person topped the university in her master's program. When people applaud her, she says that anybody could have done it. Or if a person gets promoted and her colleagues congratulate her, she says that people get promoted every year and it's not a big deal.

We need to receive strokes to live. A stroke is a single unit of attention—something that makes us feel noticed. A person criticizing us is giving us a negative stroke whereas a person praising us is giving us a positive one. We all like to believe we are good at what we do. If we routinely reject positive strokes we could feel unworthy of appreciation.

Jumping to Conclusions

As the name suggests, this distortion is about drawing conclusions without sufficient evidence. People assume the negative aspects of their situations and worry about them. This distortion can further be divided into two categories:

1. Mind reading

2. Fortune telling

Let's look at each of them:

1. Mind reading

In this type of distortion, people believe they know what others are thinking. If their assumptions go unchallenged, it could result in a parallel universe in which they draw conclusions about everybody, based on little or no evidence. They will not be able to distinguish between facts and imagination. They will respond to others based on what they believe they think, leading to complications in their relationships.

Belief: I know what you are thinking and you should know what I am thinking too.

David and Tom are friends and classmates studying in college. In one of their classes, their teacher asks them to prepare for their exams from a book. When they search for the book in stores, they realize it is unavailable. Luckily, Tom has an older edition of the book which could give him a head start in the exam preparation. David wonders if Tom will lend him the book. After some thought, he concludes that Tom will not because he knew that he needed it and didn't offer it.

David discovers a library where the book is available. Unfortunately, it is at the other end of town and has a steep subscription fee too. David joins the library and loans the book. One day, Tom gets to know about the trouble David had to go through, and feels sorry for him. He tells David that he would have loaned him the book, if only he had asked.

David assumed that Tom wouldn't lend him the book (which is a mind-read). Not only did David read Tom's mind, he expected Tom to read his mind too. He believed that if Tom could not anticipate his needs, it meant he didn't plan to help.

This kind of *I know and you should also know* thinking can lead to mind games. The expectations from others aren't communicated clearly, leading to frustration and disappointment.

Challenge: David's thinking can be challenged by asking the following questions-

How do you know that Tom would not lend you the book? Did you ask him for it?

How do you know that Tom is aware of your needs?

While pondering over these questions David might realize that he can't know what other people are thinking unless he verifies it with them. Also, they will not know his needs, unless stated explicitly.

To delve a little deeper, what is the worst that could have happened if David had asked Tom for the book? He might have refused. Nothing much more than that, I suppose. If so, it will help David to work on his fear of hearing *no*. The *fight or flight* response might be unduly kicking in, similar to when a person chooses to escape a perceived threat as it is the easiest thing to do.

We come across similar episodes of mind reading in our day-to-day life. If you meet somebody who doesn't return your smile, you might believe that the person doesn't like you. This is a mind-read. There is no evidence to back that claim, but the feeling is real.

The expectation that people should be able to read our mind, is usually linked to our childhood. Our parents knew when we were sad, even if we didn't tell them.

They were able to observe our body language and guess how we were feeling. This, sometimes, becomes an unsaid expectation in adulthood—*if you really loved me, you would know how I feel.* Such beliefs cause misunderstandings with people who love us because, despite best attempts, no one really knows what another is thinking.

Mind reading is a poor communication strategy.

2. Fortune telling

Fortune telling is the tendency to predict negative outcomes based on little or no factual data. For instance, Suzy, who we saw in the section on over-generalization, thought she would never find a partner because of three failed relationships. This is an example of fortune-telling; she believes she can look into the future.

Belief: Something bad is going to happen.

Example: *I woke up late, so I am going to have a bad day.*

Challenge: *Has this prediction been 100% accurate in the past? Have you **always** had a bad day when you woke up late?*

This is a generalization of a past event to imagine a negative event in the future.

I once knew a lady who had a tiff with her manager. She said that he was going to tell the other team members about their issues and give her a poor rating in her appraisal. I checked with her about how she could be so sure of what was going to happen. She couldn't tell.

When negative beliefs are closely held they feel like facts. They make us look into the future anxiously. Momentarily, we forget that, despite our best attempts, we can't accurately predict the future.

Should Syndrome

This distortion is prominent in people who frequently use words such as should, must, have to, or ought to. They pressurize themselves and everybody around them. They might not realize that the word *should* is loaded with expectations—how they should be, how others should be, and how the world should be. A long list of expectations makes it easy for them to fall short and feel inadequate. Others aren't able to match up either, leading to constant frustration.

In my coaching sessions, I have a mental counter that automatically increments every time my clients use the word *should*. If used frequently, it might be an area of work. They might have a rigid worldview. The mismatch between their mental picture of how things *should be* and how things *are* could cause them stress. They will gain control over their issues by working on their inflexibility rather than trying to change their external situations.

Belief: There is only one right way to do anything.

Bella was job hunting. She applied to a few companies that were looking for a candidate with a profile similar to hers. Things clicked, and she immediately got two great offers. She evaluated the benefits of joining each of them by going through the website of her potential employers, evaluating the company's past performance, and speaking to people who work there to understand their experience. After extensive research, she took up one of the offers.

In six months, Bella was disappointed with her new job. The company was not performing as she expected, her salary seemed lower than what was promised on paper, and she didn't like the company culture either.

Bella was mad at herself for not being able to predict this outcome. She recalled the other job offer in despair and perceived it as a missed opportunity. Eventually, she concluded that she is bad at making decisions.

When Bella blames herself for not being able to see the future, it makes her lose confidence in her decision-making skills. She assumes that the other job would have been better for her, although there is no way to prove that. The only way to know how that job would have been was to do it.

Challenge: Questions to Bella-

How can you know that a job isn't good for you before you take it up? Is it possible for you to know everything beforehand?

How do you know that the job you turned down would not have been worse for you?

Making big decisions could be nerve-racking for anybody. Even if we were to put a lot of effort into deciding, we could face undesirable consequences. Recall a decision that didn't work out for you. You will find some information pertaining to that decision that you didn't have when you were making it. This happens because our efforts are in the present but the results are in the future. The time lag between the two can't be bridged—ever.

When things go wrong, be gentle with yourself. Remember, you are always doing your best.

A *should* is like a personal commandment that we must live up to otherwise we feel guilty. When others don't live up to our *shoulds* we experience anger, frustration, and resentment toward them. This happens because we don't appreciate the fact that, just like us, others have a *should list* too (one that may or may not match ours).

Imagine your life to be a road on which you're traveling. The more the number of *shoulds*, the narrower your path, thus, the easier it is to fall off that path. A better way would be to stop should-ing oneself and allow things to be. This would make it easier on others too. We don't mean to encourage complacency. We will push ourselves out of our comfort zone to achieve our goals without stumbling on the *should* blocks.

Should-ing creates rigidity which hinders goal achievement. It limits a person's ability to be creative and think out-of-the-box. Most leadership coaching programs emphasize the importance of flexibility for success. It helps people adapt quickly to changing scenarios and stay afloat during challenging times.

If you tend to *should* a lot and want to reduce it, you can start by changing the structure of your sentences. Instead of saying, "I *should* wake up at 5 am and jog," you can say, "*It would be nice* if I could wake up at 5 am and jog." Giving yourself space to consider how this suggestion is good for you will work better for getting you what you want.

The intention of doing this is to reduce the number of *shoulds*, not to eliminate them. I realize that there are situations where *shoulds* are required even though they create pressure. For instance, the principal of a school might say to his students that they **should** be in school by 9 am. He wouldn't tell them **it would be nice** if they could come by 9. The rule is intended to discipline them, not invite them to a party.

I attended a training program in psychotherapy about six years ago. Eight months into the program, my should-counter was running at zero. It was interesting to see how none of my trainers—who were psychotherapists—had used the word even once. Finally, it happened. In the middle of a lecture, as I was taking down notes, I heard my trainer use *the word*. I looked up from my book, surprised. She quickly rephrased her sentence to drop the *should* out, and continued. I smiled to myself. This happens. We might know that the word *should* creates pressure, yet we might use it unconsciously. It's okay, as long as we are doing our best to use it in moderation.

Magnification or Minimization

This distortion is observed when people magnify or minimize their experience, representing it to themselves disproportionately.

1. Magnification:

Magnification happens when we see things far bigger than they are. It could cause us to exaggerate situations, such as our faults or someone else's achievements. For instance, a player who misses a shot might say to herself that she is responsible for her team losing the game. This might not be true. She is probably magnifying the impact of her missed shot on the game. There could be other reasons for her team losing the game. Similarly, if they win the game she might credit the victory to another player's performance and discount her contribution to their success.

Belief: Things are bigger than they appear to be.

Mark is traveling to another city to meet a potential client. This meeting is crucial for his organization and he ensures that he is fully prepared for it. Unfortunately, on his way to the airport, he gets stuck in traffic. He imagines that he will miss his flight, his client will refuse to reschedule the meeting, and will never work with him again. His stressful thoughts snowball uncontrollably.

When Mark reaches the airport, he is relieved to know that he hasn't missed his flight, although he was the last one to board. He reaches his destination on time. The next day, his meeting goes off well. He is delighted at his success. While returning to the airport, he muses at the imaginary negative scenarios he had while driving to the airport the previous day.

Challenge: When stuck in traffic, Mark was catastrophizing—imagining the worst possible outcome. His stressful thoughts could have been challenged by asking him-

How do you know you are going to miss your flight?

Even if you do, how are you sure your client will not be willing to reschedule?

*Is it certain that if you miss a meeting, the client will **never** want to work with you again?*

When we catastrophize, one negative thought leads to another, which quickly makes a mountain out of a molehill. The automatic negative thoughts that stem from our unconscious mind are hard to turn off. Acknowledging them is the first step toward entering a resourceful state of mind. Once that happens, we can challenge our thoughts to see the situation for what it is.

2. Minimization

Minimization is about seeing things as smaller or less significant than they are. For instance, Bella—from Should Syndrome—did extensive research on her new job before joining it. Yet, when she was dissatisfied with her job, she blamed herself for making a poor decision. If she believes that she didn't do sufficient research before selecting her job, it could be her way of minimizing the effort she had put in.

Sometimes, when we are upset with the result of our decisions, we do this as well. We unconsciously minimize the effort we/others have put in and blame ourselves/them for the outcome.

Our mind has the ability to expand and shrink experiences based on our beliefs and our current state.

People who disqualify the positive tend to minimize the importance of their achievements; people who brag are usually magnifying it. An average player might magnify and think of her achievements as greater than they are, whereas an excellent player might minimize her achievements to believe they are less significant than they are. What the player *thinks* does not accurately reflect her capability.

Four years ago, I met a girl whose parents had recently separated. She wanted to live with her mother and sister, but the situation demanded she stayed with her father. To join him, she had to relocate and enroll in a new school. She missed her mother and sister very much. She would say-

"I feel bad for such small things. I miss my mother and sister, but that doesn't mean I should stay hung up over it. I should have the ability to move on. This is life. Things happen. I should be strong."

Belief: Things are smaller than they appear to be.

Challenge: My questions for her were-

*Are the things you mentioned really that **small**?*

After everything you endured, don't you think you are already quite strong?

Parents separating, staying away from her mother and sister, and relocating, are not *small* things. When she minimizes them, she expects more from herself—like the ability to move on quickly—in order to qualify as strong. She was *should-ing* her way to stress by discounting the magnitude of the situation.

I suggested that her inner talk needs to be gentle during stressful times, such as-

"I miss my mother and sister. Anybody in my place would have felt this way. Parents separating, relocating to a new place, and joining a new school, are significant changes. I will need to be patient with myself until I find my feet. I have bravely faced so much. I am strong."

Seeing things proportionate to the way they are helped her feel better, almost instantly.

Labeling

Belief: Experiences are generic and can be labeled.

Labeling is an extreme form of over-generalization. It usually entails passing value judgment on oneself/others based on negative experiences. If we label ourselves as irresponsible, incompetent, or impatient, we manifest those behaviors in ourselves. Let's say, a student calls herself a *loser* because she failed a class. Failing a class does not make her a *loser*. Labeling herself that way could cause an emotional reaction in her which could further prevent her from performing well.

The labels we give ourselves are identity-level statements that impact our self-image positively or negatively, based on their nature.

This also applies to our perception of other people. We unconsciously view people by the labels we give them. This energy reaches them, and they react in ways to confirm our belief. For instance, if I were to call someone a miser, every time she tries to save money I might affirm to myself that she is miserly, overlooking the possibility of her having good reasons to do so. My thought process is likely to damage our relationship. Even if there was a slim chance of her spending more money, now she won't.

When we label people, the associated energy gets subconsciously communicated to them, reinforcing the labeled behavior.

Challenge: We can challenge labels by shifting them from the *identity* of the person to the *activity* being performed. The person who failed a class and called herself a loser can be challenged this way-

*What about everything you have achieved until now? Is failing a class enough to call yourself a **loser**?*

What skills do you need to create the results you want?

These questions are directed to remove the label of a loser (identity) and move it toward what needs to be done to create the results she wants (activity).

Try this out now. Think of one label you give yourself that makes you feel bad about yourself. Change it to an action. For example, if you think of yourself as *impatient,* ask yourself what you need to *do* more patiently.

Label yourself in ways that benefit you.

Challenge only negative labels you give yourself/others because it limits your worldview and creates stress. The ones that work for you don't need to be changed. For instance, some people call themselves *fitness freaks* and that helps them stay fit. Such labels can be left as they are.

Personalization

In this form of distortion, people find a way to blame themselves for negative external events, even if they aren't the primary cause for them. This might restrain them from making further attempts. For instance, a lady hosts a party and forgets to arrange some good music. She feels guilty, believing she is responsible for her guests not having a good time. Even if they didn't have a good time, there could be other factors contributing to their experience. She isn't responsible for their feelings since she doesn't control them.

People who personalize tend to link negative outcomes to themselves, however unrelated. For example, if an employee doesn't get her annual wage hike, she could believe that it happened because her manager doesn't like her. She is mind reading, along with personalizing her experience. The salary hike might not have happened for other reasons—like the company not meeting its targets. Likewise, if someone doesn't respond to your messages, it doesn't mean she doesn't like you. She might be preoccupied with difficulties of her own. If you think it is about you, then you could have taken her lack of response personally. Haven't we all received a delayed response to our messages, over which we fretted?

If people get angry with you, it doesn't reflect anything about you, although it might be easy to doubt yourself when that happens. In my practice, I have noticed that people who get angry and irritated frequently have some underlying issues that are unaddressed. It rarely has anything to do with the ones taking the heat.

If the recipients of a person's anger think it is about them, they might have taken their experience personally.

Most of what happens in the world has nothing to do with you. People have unique personality traits. They also carry the baggage of hurt, pain, and negative emotions, which they might dump on you from time to time in a manner that seems unfair. See it for what it is —their inability to conduct themselves. Their behavior is not about you. Even if they don't like something about you, they always had the option of communicating it respectfully.

Treating others poorly is optional. There is no good excuse for bad behavior.

Belief: The negative event happened because of me.

Challenge: This can be challenged by asking questions such as-

How do you know the event happened because of you?

What are the other reasons it could have happened?

Many moons ago, I was rehearsing for a dance performance with a group of colleagues, for our company's annual day. One week before the event, we went costume shopping. We were excited about exploring the new fashion street in town. After a few hours, our excitement wore out. We couldn't find a costume that we all liked. We were divided about the colors, designs, texture of the fabric, etc.

Toward the end of the day, we found a shop that had a fabulous set of costumes that fitted in with our requirements. The girls changed into them quickly and started their ramp walk. I was happy that we could finally call it a day. I asked the store manager for my size and he disappeared for half an hour. On return, he said my size was unavailable. Maybe we could look at some other designs.

We were too tired to see anything else and returned home gloomily. I felt responsible for the disappointment of my teammates. One of my friends understood how I felt. She told me not to take things personally. Unwanted situations happen, despite our best efforts. Why blame anyone?

Emotional Reasoning

After any of the distortions in thinking, emotional reasoning could follow automatically. People who reason emotionally assume that their emotions represent the way things are. This is used to draw erroneous conclusions and strengthen false beliefs.

Belief: I feel it; therefore, it must be so.

Feelings change quickly. They cannot be a basis to create one's *facts*. For instance, a lady feels jealous that her husband is paying attention to another lady. She believes he has feelings for her. Her feeling that way does not make it so.

Challenge: The following questions can be helpful to her-

How do you know your husband has feelings for her?

Does his giving attention to someone necessarily mean anything more than that?

When people are gripped by a strong emotion they selectively look for information in their environment that strengthens it. Their emotion supports their reasoning, rather than the other way around.

Overlapping Distortions

As you might have noticed, distortions overlap in many cases. A person who is disqualifying the positive is also minimizing; a person who is labeling is also over-generalizing. The distortions don't need to be mutually exclusive. They have been categorized to help us catch our unhelpful thinking styles, not to know *exactly* which distortion we are experiencing. As long as we can spot the distortion and work on it, the effort is worthwhile.

Please note:

You might be able to notice some of these distortions in others as well. Even if your observation is accurate, it will not be helpful to you as you can't control others. Hence, it is recommended that you leverage this information to change your unhelpful distortions. If you are working as a coach/therapist, you can use it to guide your clients as well.

Exercise

Study the following cases and spot the distortions in thinking:

Case 1: Betsy, a college student, enrolled in a course that taught five subjects. Although she was falling behind in one, the faculty member asked her to continue with the other four, saying that she could always catch up on the fifth subject over the year. Betsy, however, decided to drop out of the course and attend it the next year so that she could study all five subjects together. As time passed, she didn't get an opportunity to do the course. She felt disappointed, thinking she didn't get a fair chance.

Case 2: Neena feels left out in her group of friends with whom she has lunch every day. She feels disappointed because they are not mindful of her feelings while conversing. She thinks people should not interrupt or contradict her when she speaks. They should only talk about topics that interest everybody on the table.

Case 3: Pat's manager called him for a meeting without communicating the agenda. This made him anxious. He imagined that his manager would make unreasonable demands on his time or reprimand him for not achieving his targets so far.

None of what he thought happened. Much to his relief, his manager was just looking to hire a new member on the team and wanted some recommendations from him.

Distortions:

Case 1: Betsy has an All or Nothing distortion. She could have continued the course with four subjects and caught up on the fifth one later, but she decided to do all of them or none at all.

Case 2: Neena has a Should Syndrome—a list of things people should do so she doesn't feel left out. Since people might not be aware of her *shoulds*, or care enough to change, her problems at the lunch table will continue until she drops a few items off her list.

Case 3: Pat has jumped to the conclusion that his manager would make unreasonable demands on his time or show that he has failed to achieve his targets. He is mind reading by guessing his manager's agenda and catastrophizing by imagining it to be a negative one. If he stops magnifying his situation, he can see it for what it is—a meeting.

8

DEALING WITH DISTORTIONS

Even if we are aware of the concept of distortions, we will continue to distort information because the process happens unconsciously. We can't deal with the millions of bits of information we face every day. To make it more manageable, we give our own meaning to the information, delete some of it, and generalize the rest.

When faced with a stressful situation, our emotions undergo a shift. This could increase our distortion in thoughts. For instance, a person might catastrophize habitually by imagining worst-case scenarios. This tendency is likely to increase under stress.

The more time you spend gripped by negative emotions, the more distorted your version of reality is.

If you are angry, frustrated, disappointed, etc. for a long time you create a distorted perception of the situation that triggered you; moving one step away from reality every passing day. People who have a strategy to change their internal interpretation quickly and move on, suffer from less skewed perspectives.

The knowledge of distortions helps us catch our unhealthy distortions and change them in order to enter a resourceful state. Initially, we might need to put in some effort to do this consciously. With practice, it will become a part of our unconscious process and lead to a new habitual thinking style that is more useful to us. Here are a few ways to achieve that.

Write

It is easier to spot a distortion in others than in ourselves. When you are stressed about a situation, you are operating at the level of the problem. Hence, it could be difficult for you to view your thoughts objectively.

One simple way to clear your mind is to journal your thoughts. Writing will give you the distance you need from your thoughts in order to process them. If you take a break and revisit your writing in a different frame of mind, you are more likely to catch your distortions. You can do this with the list of distortions handy.

Journaling on a daily basis can help you examine your thoughts over an extended period. This is an excellent way to challenge your unhelpful beliefs and replace them with supportive ones. (Download your free copy of the **Being Yourself Journal** at romasharma.com)

Challenge

When we examined the various distortions in thinking each of them had a section called **Challenge** which had questions useful in challenging that distortion. These questions were crafted to recover information that was lost due to unconscious filtering. Once you recover this information, you will spot the distortions yourself. A shift in your perspective will result in a subsequent shift in your feelings.

While the questions that can elicit lost information are contextual, here are two generic questions that can be helpful in most situations:

1. *How do you know?* will eliminate any assumptions you have made.

Examples:

How do you know your manager doesn't like you?

How do you know your project is going to fail before you work on it?

How do you know you will never find a partner of your choice?

2. *What does that mean?* will help you reflect on your interpretation of the situation.

Examples:

What does not getting a promotion mean to you?

What does her not paying attention mean?

What does a past project not working out mean?

Once the thought has been challenged, it can be replaced with a new, more helpful thought to create a different emotion. Without substitution, it will go unaddressed, only to spring up later in a different situation.

A Note to Counselors on Challenging:

1. Information Vs Discovery

If you have ever been told what to do and it didn't resonate with you, you know how it feels. Even if you listen to the person you will internally reject his/her views. Information isn't helpful, discovery is.

If you are working as a coach, avoid spending time trying to get the type of distortion right. It is enough if you can spot the distortion and challenge it. You might know what your clients need to do to resolve their issues. However, *telling* them isn't as helpful as *enabling* them to discover their solutions for themselves.

2. Respectful Reflection

While challenging your client, your tonality and body language need to convey respect, otherwise it could break rapport. People who are hurt because of being challenged are usually feeling judged or rejected. This prevents them from sharing information, wasting time and effort put into the session.

3. Readiness

You could also experience resistance if the person is not ready to be challenged. Sometimes, people are not looking for solutions, they need something else—to pour out, to feel heard, or to be acknowledged. It helps to give them what they need in the moment.

Challenge a person's thought process only when he/she is ready for it.

The same applies to you. Use a gentle tonality and encouraging words with yourself. If one or both of your parents were critical in your growing years, take care not to sound like them when correcting your distortions. The intention of this exercise is to feel better by working on your distortions, not to put yourself down (people who identify with the *Should Syndrome* need to take special care of this).

Exercise

Pick an event that usually sends you into an un-resourceful state (such as sad, angry, or scared) and fill the table below. Detect your distortions and challenge them.

Event	Emotion	Automatic Negative thought	Distortion(s) in thinking	Alternative thought	Emotion
I made a mistake at work.	Scared, Disappointed	I might lose my job.	Jumping to conclusions, Magnifying	Everyone makes mistakes from time to time. I have learnt something useful from this experience.	Calm, Relaxed

Challenge Your Distortions

Reframe

A frame provides a context to our thinking. When we feel stuck in a situation, the frame in which we operate keeps us focused on the problem—what isn't right, what caused it, etc.—or helps us find solutions such as what can be done and what resources we have to do it. (For more details on Frames of Thinking, please refer to my book, Thinking Habits For Definite Success.)

A situation might not necessarily be a *problem*. It could have a positive side that is eluding us because of what we have decided to focus on. A reframe is a single-step interrupt designed to improve our mental state when we are experiencing a negative emotion. It helps us feel better by changing our interpretation of the situation.

Reframing our difficult situations creates more choices for us.

Suppose you greet your colleague in a warm and friendly manner, but she ignores you. You might feel angry, assuming her to be a snobbish person. Later in the day, someone tells you that she lost a loved one that morning. Suddenly, you are sorry for her. You no longer find her snobbish. You might even experience remorse for having thought that way.

When we change the frame, we change the meaning and the subsequent feeling.

It is easier for us to understand our own frames than that of others, making them a good starting point for change.

Content Reframe

A content reframe changes the interpretation of a situation by working on different aspects of the content to bring out a silver lining.

For example:

1. *My manager gives me a lot of work to do. I'm sure she doesn't like me.*

Reframe: Maybe your manager trusts you so much and that's why she gives you more work to do.

2. My mother is so busy planning my sister's wedding. She gives a lot of attention to my sister and doesn't care for me anymore.

Reframe: Maybe your mother is giving more attention to your sister because she is moving away after her marriage and she will see less of her.

Similarly, you can reframe your difficult situations by checking-

What is the positive aspect of this situation?

Let's take another example. A wife is angry with her husband working late at the office. His intention behind spending less time with her could be to earn more money so they can have a better living. That might be a frame she has not considered.

We are not deluding ourselves by looking for positives. There might be an angle we have not yet considered—one that could make us feel better—because every story has two sides, and every behavior has an unconscious positive intention.

Context Reframe

Another way to look at the upside of a situation is by changing the context. A context reframe is based on the premise that a behavior which is unwanted in one scenario could be a blessing in another. Unlike content reframe, here, we change the context of the situation to gain a fresh perspective.

For example:

1. *My child is very rough and tough.*

Reframe: Can you think of a situation where this behavior might be useful? Maybe if somebody bullies her it might help her stand up for herself.

2. *My role at the office is demanding and very stressful.*

Reframe: Dealing with stress at this position will help you manage the stress you will experience at leadership positions.

3. My son plays too much cricket.

Reframe: You might have the next budding international cricketer in your house.

Similarly, you can reframe other situations by checking-

In which context can the current behavior be useful?

Are you likely to experience that context in the future?

Please note:

Reframing helps us counter a negative distortion with a positive one. However, we do not reframe to distract ourselves from problems by creating imaginary positive scenarios or to encourage inactivity. If your job is too stressful or your manager is giving you more work than you can handle, you might need to address it. The reframe is to change your state of mind to a resourceful one so that you can make effective decisions on what to do next.

Humor Reframe

You might have observed, at times, that when people talk about their problems they eventually start laughing at what they are saying. Humor is known to weaken the neurological structure of a problem. If you change your perspective, you are likely to find something funny about it.

If you are reframing for someone else using humor, ensure you have a rapport with the person and he/she is in the right mood. If you don't have a rapport, don't force it. You might have a good reframe up your sleeve but, without the readiness of the recipient, it will not work.

A few years ago, I met the sales head of a certain company, who said to me-

"My employee duped me. He divulged details of my tender to my competitor and we lost the deal. I was trying to create a core committee of trusted members to take the company forward and this is the kind of person I chose. I am not smart enough."

I asked him to role play his situation with me—I am the employee who cheated him, and he is himself. I approached him and said that I am responsible for the deal not coming through. He tried looking at me angrily, but he couldn't and started smiling.

I murmured, "You look too happy for a person who just found out that his employee gave him away. I tried to escape, but you outsmarted me. Good job ratting me out, although I wish you were late by a bit. I always dreamt of being on that committee."

By this point, he was in splits. He suddenly didn't seem to feel as bad about his situation. He agreed that if he was going to filter people out, this episode happened timely. His current loss was insignificant compared to the potential loss of having a fraudulent person on the committee.

A Quality Reframe

Reframing applies only to certain situations and needs to be done judiciously. It works best when you are ready for it. If you find yourself resisting a reframe, drop it for the time being and try a different approach later. We know that a reframe has worked if you feel better at the end of it. If you are reframing for someone else, you will see a positive shift in their non-verbal communication, indicating it has worked. Look out for a change in posture, such as relaxed shoulders, deep breathing, or smiling.

When I teach reframing in my training programs, sometimes participants give me examples from their lives which they can't reframe. My usual response is that it is not necessary—nor is it even possible—to reframe *all* scenarios in life. A reframe is like a tool in a toolkit that needs to be used appropriately. If we use a hammer when we need a spanner, it won't work. If you humor a person with whom you don't have a rapport, or show a positive side to a situation that doesn't feel positive, the reframe could backfire.

If you feel like something positive exists—even if it is unknown—you can attempt to reframe the situation. If it can't be reframed, don't *try* to do it. We don't want to introduce a positive distortion in a way that could potentially create more problems. For example, if a person says, "I smoke a lot," it might not be helpful to say, "That's okay, at least you are breathing." We can put a positive spin on almost anything, but it needs to align well with the overall outcome.

Exercise

Think of a problem you are facing currently. Check if you can reframe it using the frames mentioned above. If you can find a person who is interested in doing this exercise, you both can write your situations on a sheet of paper, swap your sheets once you are done, and reframe for each other. Then, take your sheets back and check if the reframe has helped you.

You can do the same for yourself, but doing it with others can give you better results. Since they aren't a part of the problem, they might give you a unique perspective on your situation.

Please note:

The person you are doing this exercise with also needs to understand the concept of reframing. So, you will need to share this section or explain it to him/her. Choose a mild problem to work on (unless you are working with a trained professional).

9

CHANGE YOUR FEELING

Mental Movies

Your mind is the screen on which you cast your movies. Based on the reel you project, you experience your feelings. When you play the movie of a time when someone abused you, you feel angry; or the time when you got your first pet, you feel happy. The quality of the movie also impacts your feelings. If you watch a horror movie in a theatre, you feel scared because of the loud sounds and enormous images. However, if you were to see the same movie on your mobile phone, it might not scare you as much.

Likewise, people who are depressed play big, bright movies of things that hurt them in the foreground of their mind, like when they were treated poorly, or didn't succeed in their outcomes. These mental movies play like the ones in theatres—with surround sound and high definition picture quality—resulting in intense emotions. Their happy days play less frequently and far away from their mind. These movies don't have clear picture quality or sound effects. Hence, they don't create positive feelings with as much intensity as the negative ones.

The way you talk to yourself and the mental movies you play will largely decide how you feel.

People who constantly focus on what's missing and interpret situations negatively get into the habit of being miserable. Over time, they get better at it. This could cause them to create unhelpful generalizations about their life, leading to despair.

Focus + Interpretation = Feeling State

By challenging distortions and reframing, you can change both your focus and interpretation to create positive feelings. Changing either of them also works, but it is recommended to do both for best results. Just changing your focus sometimes serves as a distraction. When you return to the situation, if your interpretation is the same, your feeling will be the same too.

In the previous sections, we have gone over ways to change our thoughts in order to change our feelings. Now, let's look at the other way around—how we can change our feelings to change our thoughts.

Accepting and labeling

If you are experiencing an unpleasant emotion and would like to change it, the first step is to accept it wholeheartedly. Acknowledge how you are feeling without judging yourself for it. If you judge, you are effectively telling yourself that you are not okay the way you are. This will increase the intensity of the problem.

Rejecting feelings is like rejecting reality.

Give the feeling a name. How are you feeling—angry, disappointed, frustrated, or scared? Labeling your feelings separates them from you.

Instead of saying:

"I am angry."

say:

"I am experiencing anger."

There is a difference between experiencing a feeling and blending it into yourself. Wording it differently will create a natural distance that will help you feel better.

Disassociation

If you are physically in a situation, and seeing it through your eyes, you are associated with it. When you look at yourself outside your situation, you are disassociated from it. For instance, if you imagine seeing yourself on a roller coaster you are disassociated, whereas if you imagine yourself *on* the roller coaster, seeing the ride through your eyes, you are associated with the experience.

When you are happy, you are fully associated with the people in your environment. This helps you enjoy life and feel your emotions to the fullest. However, there are times when you are stressed and want to gain some distance from your uncomfortable emotions. This is when it helps to disassociate from them.

Association increases the intensity of the emotion, whereas disassociation reduces it.

The disassociation exercise aims to remove you from the situation so you can see it without the emotional charge it carries. It is a useful *state change tool* when you are overwhelmed by a situation and are looking for a way forward.

Step 1: Blow the problem out of your mind along with the emotions it carries, with a pushing-out hand movement and a quick strong exhale through the mouth.

Step 2: Look at the point where you exhaled your problem. Walk around it, looking at it from different angles. Observe what you are doing in this scene. What are others doing? What do you want in this situation?

Step 3: Walk a few steps away from the scene. Look back at it. How do you feel? Walk further away and look back. How do you feel now?

Step 4: What is the positive intention behind your behavior in this scene? Is there a behavior that will satisfy the same intention better?

Step 5: Imagine yourself exhibiting the new behavior. Step into the situation. How do you feel about it now?

Step 6: Step out of the situation and shake it off.

Blowing your problem out of your mind will disassociate you from it. Looking at the problem from a disassociated perspective can give you solutions that might not have occurred to you when you were in an unresourceful state. The same thing happens when you are able to come up with more solutions for a friend's problem than your own. As we saw in the section, Effect of Mood on Thoughts, our mood tries to sustain itself. The mood loop can be broken by doing the disassociation exercise.

In my training programs, I have noticed that trainees instantly feel better when they disassociate from their problem. If you have a coach who can guide you through the exercise, it is better, as then you can focus on your process. If you are planning to do the exercise on your own, ensure you have space and privacy. Either way, don't pressurize yourself to find alternate solutions. Sometimes, all you need to do to feel better is to step out of the problem, then solutions follow on their own.

Physiology

It is difficult to have a healthy mind in an unhealthy body, or the other way around, because your mind and body are a part of the same system—whatever impacts one, impacts the other. Hence, while trying to create good feelings, it is necessary to work on both aspects of yourself.

Your health is a silent underlying contributor to your mood. It makes you enjoy life or struggle with it. If you haven't eaten well or slept enough, you tend to feel irritated. Your willpower is low. You find it difficult to concentrate and generate the results you want. People around you seem more careless than usual. However, if you are feeling fit, you might ignore their mistakes and not perceive them as careless. The people in both situations are the same. You feel differently based on your level of fitness.

Nurses in hospitals are trained to deal with the moods of their patients. People who are sick are more likely to get irritated because their bodies aren't able to handle the stress. Dealing with them requires patience.

Medical research shows that people with vitamin and mineral deficiencies show signs of depression. Even people who have high blood pressure, hormonal imbalance, low sugar, or chemical imbalance have symptoms like anger, irritability, mood swings, etc. In such cases, just working on the person's distortions and trying to reframe situations doesn't help because the biochemistry is sustaining the mood.

There are a variety of medical reasons that impact your physiology and prevent you from feeling happy. When coaching or counseling doesn't help, and there are other symptoms—such as lack of sleep, constant fatigue, crying spells, or bouts of anger—it might be necessary for the person to get a health checkup. The biochemistry might have been harmed by the person's thinking patterns. Regardless of which end the problem started, it needs to be addressed to break the cybernetic loop.

In my practice, I have found that when counselors approach seniors to review a case that isn't progressing, almost 30% of the time it requires a transfer to a doctor. If counselors and coaches are not trained to detect and redirect clients when required—or they miss doing so—the sessions go on forever, almost fruitlessly.

If you feel that working on your beliefs, challenging your distortions, reframing, and other coaching methods are not helping and your body feels strained, it is recommended to rule out the possibility of health issues by consulting a medical professional.

Ensure your lifestyle prioritizes taking good care of yourself. This includes eating nutritious food, exercising, meditating, doing yoga and other activities that promote fitness. Drink plenty of water during the day, sleep for 7-8 hours at night, and take rest when your body asks for it. These simple practices are often ignored, resulting in tiredness and stress.

Your body needs to be in alliance with your mind to solve your problems. You might have noticed that when your breathing is shallow or you are experiencing palpitations due to anxiety, you can't find the solutions you are looking for.

To change your feeling, instead of working on your psychology it helps to first work on your physiology.

If you are stressed, go for a walk, meditate, do breathing exercises or anything else that relaxes you. Once you calm down, you can work on your thoughts.

10

DEALING WITH BAD MEMORIES

It is an instinct for us to live in the moment, just like babies and animals. If we are unable to do so, there is probably something unresolved in our subconscious mind that is stopping us.

If you feel like a bad memory is hijacking your present moment, don't ignore, it even if it seems like the easiest thing to do. If we have weeds growing in our garden, they will not go away by affirming positively that they do not exist. Work is required to de-weed the garden and get rid of the toxic plants that take away resources from the other plants we are trying to grow.

Sometimes, when people don't want to face their fears, they use drugs or alcohol to numb their pain, which isn't helpful either. It is like de-weeding the garden by cutting off the weeds by the head; they grow back in no time. To get rid of them, they will need to be uprooted, otherwise, even if they are pushed down they will keep growing.

Forgiveness

If you've ever had difficulty forgiving someone you might remember how it brought you down. Medical research has provided us with sufficient evidence to understand the damaging effects of resentment on the body. Resenting a person is like drinking poison and hoping that the other person dies. We are not figuratively drinking poison, it is literally, because of the chemicals that are released in our body when we resent someone.

The person who hurt you is probably going about his/her life unconcerned, while you suffer as you replay your bad memories—the public humiliation, the additional work that was enforced on you, or the long-term trauma you were subjected to because someone cared very little. *"You should forgive others for your own good,"* is easy to say but is difficult for people to do, especially if someone wronged them severely. If they truly cared for the person, it is much harder.

Forgiving people is work. It is not about someone rationalizing and telling you *their* reasons for *you* to forgive. The instinct to get even with people is natural. Trying to suppress it only strengthens it.

If you are suffering because someone inflicted pain on you, the best way forward would be to connect with *your* reasons to forgive the person. Think about how your life will be better once you are free from the pain. The decision to forgive needs to come from within. One factor that could help you reach that decision is crossing the threshold of pain. Once you realize that you have been through enough pain and can't bear it anymore, you will be motivated to look for ways to let go of it.

Check with yourself-

How much have you already suffered? Are you willing to go through it any longer?

How were your loved ones impacted by your resentment?

What benefits do you see in forgiving the person who hurt you?

Despite what others have done to you, the responsibility to take care of yourself still lies with you. Carrying your baggage through a journey can be very tiring. Put it down; there is nothing to fear. Whatever happened will equip you to handle similar situations in the future.

The event is over. What you are responding to is a memory.

Resentment Physically Exists

When people say, "You must forget and forgive," it seems easier said than done. We can't just forget our pain because it is real—an adverse response to an adverse experience. If you suffered an injury and someone said to you, "Forget about your broken bone," wouldn't it be absurd? That is exactly how it is when people ask others to forget about their resentment.

Resentment physically exists in your brain in the form of neural pathways. You will need to work to remove them, the way work went into creating them. When you revisit a painful memory, the associated neural pathways get fired, throwing open your emotional flood gates. Sometimes, even a tiny trigger is enough to set this off without warning. Your body goes through a physiological reaction. The stress releases chemicals that hurt your immune system. Your heartbeat, pulse rate, and breathing patterns change. You feel like a different person.

Going through this cycle repeatedly strengthens the associated neural pathways, changes your biochemistry and impacts your long-term health. Hence, the longer you take to forgive a person, the tougher it becomes to do so.

Exercise

Let's do an exercise to see how your resentment impacts your body. Find a partner to do this exercise with you.

Step 1: Stand straight. Hold your hand out. Think of someone you don't like.

Step 2: Ask your partner to push your hand down. You will notice that it easily goes down.

Step 3: Now think of someone you love very much. Ask your partner to push your hand down with the same force as the last time. This time your hand will be firm and won't go down easily.

In **Step 3**, if you surround the person you detest with the light of love, once again your arm will become strong. In all the above steps, your body is responding to the thought of the person. Hence, resolving your thoughts will not only help you feel better mentally, but physically as well.

In a session, before working on a problem, I always check with my clients-

Can I take this problem away? Are you ready to let go of it?

Just because we *can* take a problem away doesn't mean that we *should*. The unconscious mind has reasons for holding onto the painful memory, maybe as an act of protection. The person needs to be fully ready to let go before we can start the healing work.

When I suggest resolving painful memories, I often see my clients suddenly deny that they have a problem. Or, they defer it, saying that time will take care of things. This is a weak argument because:

1. Very often the topics we discuss in sessions are already quite old. If time had to heal them, they would have been healed by now. If their thought process didn't resolve their problems in the past and is sustained, the same outcome is likely to be created in the future as well.

2. If they think they don't have a problem at all, they are probably in denial. If a problem didn't exist, we wouldn't be discussing it. If it is bothering them, it *is* a problem, however much they might try to minimize it.

When people refuse to work on their painful memories, they are usually trying to escape their worst fears.

In coaching, most of my effort goes into establishing that nursing grudges is equivalent to suffering. It isn't an activity that can be done comfortably in the privacy of one's mind. We pay for it with our mental peace and physical fitness. If my clients ever feel the urge to turn away from it, I get them to reflect on the benefits they will have once they are free of this pain.

If you have unresolved grievances, you might need to speak to the people who hurt you, but before that, it is important to know the objective of doing so. If you want them to realize their mistake, that might not happen. Even if it does, it might not help you. The neural pathways that lead to pain are inside your mind, not theirs. So, while their admitting to their wrongdoings might ease things out for you, the work of letting go will still need to be done at your end.

When you are hurt, and don't tend to your wounds appropriately, you give birth to a person inside your mind. Let's call this person Resentment. Every time you think about the person you detest, you feed Resentment a little more. After a while, she grows bigger than you. It is hard to regulate her impact. She speaks so loudly, you can't hear your own voice. As time passes, it becomes tougher to get rid of her.

The people who hurt you might not empathize with you, because they are unaware of your situation or lack empathy. The intention of forgiving them is more for your benefit than theirs. Gently support yourself to seek closure. Check-

Do you want to say something to this person? Despite your hurt, can you bring yourself to respect this person?

Do you want to have nothing to do with this person? Can you send him/her healing vibrations, anyway?

Impacts Your Life

Holding a grudge requires a lot of mental energy to keep it in place. This assimilates in your body as pain. You take the same body to your parties, workplace, or home. The pain that lives inside you goes everywhere— impacting you and others in your environment— regardless of who caused it.

I sometimes hear people say, "I hold a grudge *only* with this person. With everyone else, things are fine." This might be true, at the same time, they need to account for how this poor relationship makes them unavailable to others.

You don't think as much about the people who love you as the ones who hurt you. When you are preoccupied, your loved ones will not get your attention. They are also likely to be at the receiving end of your pent-up anger and other unresolved emotions. As a result, they will find it difficult to have a good relationship with you.

For instance, if the lady of a house is angry at her ex-husband for leaving her, she will not be able to attend to her needs or that of her current family. If she finds a way to gain closure on her situation, she will have more mind space to love herself and others. The starting point is deciding that she wants to heal by forgiving her ex-husband and then working on her experiences to give them a new interpretation.

A grudge in one relationship spreads to others as well.

Change Your Interpretation

We are not responding to situations as much as to our interpretations of them. Even a seemingly *bad* situation has an upside to it. One that you might have missed while you were in an un-resourceful state. When a bad memory springs back, check-

What was good about this experience?

How has it contributed to your life?

Maybe being hurt made you an empathetic person. You understood the pain that someone's destructive behavior inflicted on you, and so you were careful not to do the same with others. This quality might have helped you develop deep and meaningful relationships.

Life situations are due to a person's decisions, not conditions. Even the *bad* experiences help you make better decisions in the future. They enable you to navigate through the maze of life by distinguishing what is *right* and *wrong* for you. This makes your life exactly the way you want it.

Reframe Your Memory

Painful memories are luckily just memories. As we saw in the section, Reframe, they can be reframed to feel better. You might not completely forget what happened with you but when you look back, you could feel better based on the way you choose to look at it. For instance, a lady believed that the pain her ex-boyfriend inflicted on her helped her immensely while choosing a life partner. This interpretation made her bless him when she went on to experience decades of happiness with someone else.

Similarly, a man who was constantly ill-treated by his manager gave up one day and quit his job. He found a new job and settled down in a few months. Yet, it filled him with bitterness every time he thought about his ex-manager and the trouble he had to go through switching jobs.

In his new job, he built an excellent team of people who loved to work for him because he treated them with respect. One day, he realized that he should thank his ex-manager instead of hating him because he taught him what *not* to do. Being on the receiving end of disrespect made him respect others, which paid off in the long run.

We are always learning—from the people who loved us as well as hurt us.

People who are abusive, contemptuous, or hurtful in their ways, become a source of negativity in the lives of others around them. We end up distancing ourselves from them. We have all been in situations where we couldn't take someone's behavior anymore and decided to move on. We didn't deal with it or communicate our thoughts because we didn't feel the need for it. It was just easier to walk away silently.

This might work when we are not invested in the relationship. However, it becomes harder to do when we are dealing with our loved ones—our family members, close friends, or partners. We did not choose our parents, siblings, or relatives. We cannot decide to leave this family and find a *better* family for ourselves. There are people we might want to forgive, even if past attempts have failed. Let's look at some interpretations that can help us do this.

Compassion

One way to forgive others is to understand that people are always doing their best, even if their behavior isn't the best. Happy people don't hurt others. It is only people who are hurt themselves who try to bring others down. The person who abused you has also been abused; the person who bullied you has been a victim too. It may not be due to you, but they went through the unpleasant experience and deflected it onto you.

They might have chosen you because they knew you were unlikely to hurt them back. Or maybe they had such little control over their own lives that controlling you gave them a sense of power. Whatever they did, they had an unconscious positive intention for themselves.

We don't mean to justify their behavior by thinking this way. Rationalizing bad behavior is bad behavior too. The intention is to understand their side of the story so it can help us make sense of ours. We might believe that we suffered at their hands when actually, they might be suffering too, equally, if not more. Once we see what happened to us through the lens of compassion, things become clearer to us.

Some people suffered as children at the hands of emotionally immature parents who did not behave like adults. Instead of meeting the needs of their children, they expected their children to meet their needs. These children grow up resenting their parents. They want to have a good relationship with them, but aren't able to.

Adults, who have been abused as children, feel better when they delve into the childhood of their parents. When they see that their parents suffered themselves, they find it easier to forgive them. They realize that they couldn't give them what they themselves didn't get. This interpretation helps them heal.

If you are hurt by someone, put yourself into the person's shoes and ask yourself-

What need is the person trying to satisfy?

If you were to lead his/her life, what would your challenges be?

Self-righteousness

Sometimes what you think is right might not necessarily be *right,* even if you feel strongly about it. Others might have a *right* that is different from yours. With time, age, and the influence of new people, your definition of *right* and *wrong* could also change. This could result in a different interpretation of your bad memory —one in which you might not believe you were wronged at all.

A man used to detest his mother for leaving him with a babysitter in his infancy while she went to work. As a baby, he would yearn for her and those memories made him angry with her in adulthood. His mother told him that his father made some poor business decisions, due to which they were left with no money. She had no option but to work.

Her son couldn't understand her reasons, until one day his business faced a crisis. He wondered if he could seek his wife's support to run the house. When he saw that in a similar situation he also needed a supportive wife—like his mother was to his father—his resentment melted.

There are cases where the people we resent might have done nothing worth receiving a lifetime of resentment. We feel validated in disliking them because it explains how we feel about them. It might not indicate anything about them. It is helpful to challenge any inconspicuous distortions before we decide that they were *wrong* and we were *right*.

Compassion with Boundaries

We have gone over ways to be compassionate, understand the perspective of others, and give them the benefit of doubt. Besides being compassionate, we also need to know when to call people out so that we don't play along in situations that are not in our best interest.

⁂

Ellen's husband, Dereck, was abusive. Whenever he had too much to drink, he would beat her and blame it on the alcohol. Felicia, the nurse who attended to her wounds, frequently advised her to stand up for herself —either tell him to mend his ways, or leave. Ellen was bound by her religious beliefs of not breaking relationships. She believed more in forgiveness than in her well-being. She also felt sorry for Dereck because he had been through a tough childhood and used that to justify his behavior. Every time he hit her and apologized, she forgave him. She believed him when he said that he would not repeat his behavior again, until it became the new normal.

One day, Dereck saw her speaking to another man and got wild. He hit her *accidentally,* injuring her leg. Ellen had to be hospitalized. She underwent a minor surgery and recovered in a week, though not completely. Felicia told her that she would not be able to walk without support again. Forgiveness came at a price, and this time it was steep.

Felicia advised Ellen against going back to Dereck, but Ellen said there was nothing to worry about. It was just an accident. She forgave Dereck as she interpreted the situation differently. She thought he hit her because he was jealous when he saw her talking to another man. It's okay to feel jealous. It just shows how much he loves her.

⁂

Many spiritual and religious beliefs encourage us to be compassionate and forgiving toward others. These teachings are good because they create a better world. At the same time, we need to evaluate carefully what the aftereffect of forgiving someone is.

Compassion doesn't mean inactivity. It mustn't be misunderstood for weakness either. We need to act on what is right for us and compassion gives us the strength to do that. If a person gets beaten frequently and she says it is because her husband loves her, this interpretation could cause her to forgive him and repeat the pattern all over again.

There is no compassion without boundaries.

A good interpretation is one that not only leads to good feelings but also one's well-being. If you are in a difficult relationship and you've tried everything—such as communicating your needs, understanding and meeting the person's needs—and you still face abusive behavior, it might be time to let go. This is the last option, assuming all attempts to improve the relationship over time have failed.

It is important to know when to opt out of a relationship, otherwise you could get used to the pain. In such cases, it is harder for you to leave due to a trauma bond established with the abusive person. If you decide to do so, seek support in your circle of friends and family members, and undergo sessions with a mental health professional. Focus on yourself while giving the person a healing vibration every time they cross your mind. A good internal thought process is-

I am right and so are you. I let you go. You are free to live your life and I am free to live mine too. I wish you the very best.

Guilt

Guilt is a powerful emotion that can turn our life inside out. When we believe we have done something wrong we punish ourselves by going over it repeatedly in our mind. We wonder if we can turn back time and make up for our mistakes. The anger and resentment directed toward ourselves hurts us, whether we deserve it or not. It prevents us from loving ourselves for who we are. This energy spreads to other areas of our life too. We find it difficult to have good relationships with our loved ones while we are caught up in the thoughts of what went wrong.

Forgiving ourselves is as important as forgiving others. There are things we did in the past that we might not be proud of. Whenever we relive the memory, we go through pain. Maybe we didn't stand up for ourselves when we should have, or we took a decision that impacted others adversely. Regardless of the reason, a memory that causes guilt needs to be dealt with.

Perceived Fault

If episodes from your past loom over you in the form of guilt, remember that what you thought was *wrong* might not be wrong at all. For instance, if you feel guilty for leaving a relationship, you might have accepted more responsibility than is rightfully yours, like discounting the poor treatment meted out to you by others. If there are any other negative aftereffects of the relationship falling apart—like loss of common friends, or children—you might unfairly blame yourself for that too.

Check your thoughts for distortions. If you personalize a painful event by linking it back to yourself, maximize the significance of your actions and minimize the contribution of others, you could feel guilty. Maybe you weren't at fault; somebody just made you feel that way.

Sometimes people assume responsibility for things that weren't in their control. I reflect this to people who believe that their parents would be together if they had been better as children. When they link unrelated events, they experience guilt, directing undue resentment toward themselves.

Redemption

If you have spotted any distortions in your thinking and realized that you weren't responsible for a painful episode from the past, you must already feel much lighter. However, if you believe you were at fault, then you will need to deal with the anger and resentment you are experiencing toward yourself.

We can get away from a person we detest, but when that person is *us*, we feel helpless. Even if we run away from ourselves, our feelings will catch up. We can't sweep them under the carpet and pretend they don't exist. Eventually, we will have to face them.

If you believe you hurt someone—intentionally or otherwise—and it is making you feel guilty, you will need to work through it. What needs to be done is contextual. You might seek forgiveness through your thoughts, if you believe the person will not communicate with you (or is no more). Alternately, you might choose to go up to the person and speak to them about what happened. This requires courage but might work well, especially if that's what you need to gain closure.

If apologizing isn't an option, see if there are any other amends you would like to make. Maybe you can change your behavior to reflect how you feel about what happened. To do this, you will need to find out what the person needs and give it to him/her.

I once knew a person who felt guilty for forgetting his wife's birthday. He obviously couldn't bring her birthday back, but to make amends he started spending more time with her on weekends, which helped their relationship.

Replace your regrets from the past with promising behavior for the future.

Self-compassion

Even if you seek forgiveness, people may or may not forgive you, based on where they are in their healing process. You might want to reconstruct the relationship, but they might not want the same. After you have offered your sincere apology, appreciate yourself for it because not many people are able to go through with it. Even if they continue to nurture their negativity toward you, you can give healing vibrations to yourself and them.

Forgive yourself, knowing that when you made a poor decision, you had an unconscious positive intention for yourself. You were thinking about what's best for you and didn't realize that you would regret it someday.

When presented with choices, people always pick the best one available to them.

- Virginia Satir, Psychotherapist

Here are some useful beliefs to deal with guilt:

It's okay to make a mistake.

It's okay to admit your mistake.

It's okay if others don't accept your sincere apology.

It's okay to love yourself and others with their imperfections.

The ability to humbly love yourself, even when others don't, can be incredibly empowering. Once you have made peace with yourself, create a firm resolve to do things differently in the future. This is to use what happened as a learning experience to improve your life.

Exercise

If you are ready to get rid of bad memories, here are two visualizations you can do:

1. Every time a bad memory pops up, make the screen of your mind white and replace it with a happy visualization for the future.

2. Imagine your life without your bad memories. How will it be? What will change and how will it help you?

11
─────
EGO

The Image

Your ego is an illusion that makes you believe you are separate from others. It is an attachment to a false sense of self. The word *false* implies that our identities are self-created and subject to distortion. If someone asks you who you are, you might respond based on your profession, country, religion, or just your name. These are labels. Any other person could have all these but would still not be you.

The labels you give yourself become an integral part of your identity and people have a strong need to act based on their identity. If a person thinks, "I am always right," she will need to be right at all times. Otherwise, she will feel like she doesn't know herself. Once this belief of being right merges into her identity, it will become the source of her problems.

A baby doesn't know who she is. People call out something they find unique in her and she starts believing what they say. This shapes her self-image as fat, good-looking, ugly, funny, intelligent, nitwit, etc. The greater the frequency of the reinforcement, the stronger her belief is. Her self-image struggles to cope with unrealistic messages such as:

You should never fail.

You should not make a mistake.

You should be perfect.

These messages go deep into her unconscious mind, making it hard for her to live up to her own image. If one or both of her parents had a need to always be right or had an inflated sense of self, she could unconsciously absorb that too.

A baby doesn't know that she is picking up patterns from her parents. Her programming continues to play out in adulthood. When people correct her, she feels upset because she is not supposed to make a mistake. She gets defensive and starts arguing over trivial things as it goes against her sense of self. She is worried about what people will think of her and provides detailed clarifications, even when no one was expecting it. She is more focused on protecting her image than responding to what is being said. Needless to say, this gets in the way of her relationships.

Ego develops based on:

1. How you see yourself, Self-Image

We create our unique self-image based on how we filter and perceive information available on ourselves. This image might not accurately reflect who we are; it is created based on what we *thought* is true about us. These perceptions develop our ego. We will see this in detail in the section, Self-Esteem.

2. How others see you, Public Image

Our public image is important to us. It is natural for us to feel good when we are appreciated by others. Our actions are influenced by how we will be perceived. This is why we are different when we are around people rather than by ourselves.

People feel the need to live up to what the world thinks of them—an identity others have labeled onto them. This is what makes a soldier forget that his life is at stake and face a battle, or a nurse to work in a deadly pandemic. It is natural to want a good public image. However, when the need for it becomes strong, we become overly concerned with what others think about us. Our ego gets in the way.

Which image is a strong driver?

Both self and public images develop at an early age and continue to take form as we go through life. Having a strong self-image is necessary for our happiness. It allows us to love ourselves for who we are rather than what others want us to be.

People could do things to satisfy either image of theirs. If they have a healthy self-esteem, they are likely to do it based on their self-image. They are happy, because they are not dependent on the opinions of others. When people have a low self-esteem, their actions are guided by their public image. They encounter more unhappiness, because public image is based on what others think—not something they can control. They try hard to create a good impression and feel validated by the appreciation of others. Their inauthenticity robs them of their spontaneity because what they do is not in sync with what they want to do. This mismatch leaves them feeling drained.

Ask yourself-

What is more important to you—how you see yourself or how others see you?

How congruent are your thoughts with your behavior?

If you wanted to do something that could attract the disapproval of others, would you still go ahead?

Attachment

Ego causes people to cling to things they like—appearance, money, people, etc. They have a strong need for things to be the same so they can continue enjoying them. For instance, people who feel sad when they see pictures of their younger selves, and miss how they looked back then, are attached to their appearances. This is something that is bound to change over time and will cause them disappointment along the way because they couldn't control it.

Similarly, people experience sorrow when they aren't with their loved ones anymore. They miss old times and remember how happy they were together. While missing people who aren't around is natural, clinging to them isn't. It happens when people have an unmet need for positive strokes. If a baby did not receive adequate love and attention from her parents, she might cling to a person in adulthood who meets that need.

Attachment to things causes sorrow. When things change, it creates a sense of loss. Wanting material objects such as clothes, cars, electronic goods, etc. leads to consumerism. People hoard things they don't need, and look at things they don't have with a sense of inadequacy. This can be seen in affluent people who experience remorse at losing a relatively small amount of money, because they were attached to it.

The ego keeps people mentally exalting themselves. If they believe they are rich or good-looking, they wouldn't want to let go of that image. If they do, they will be in pain. Just the thought of their skin wrinkling or their bank balance shrinking will be unbearable, even if it doesn't change their life in any way.

Accepting Change

One way to reduce the disappointment in our life is to accept that change is natural. We live knowing that what is there today might not be there tomorrow. This isn't a pessimistic mindset, but a practical one. It keeps us from feeling shocked when people suddenly stop communicating with us or liking us. It allows us to love ourselves as we age, with all the aches and pains that might exist in our body. It helps us stay calm when we lose money, knowing that it is a temporary exchange of hands and we can earn it back in a matter of time.

Accepting change doesn't imply complacency. It means that we are okay with who we are and what our life situation is. It helps us live mindfully in the present moment. Otherwise, the desire for something more keeps us striving and dissatisfied.

Constant change has an upside that people often miss—the things that cause us to suffer *also* change. If you find your job, people, or circumstances difficult, they could all change for the better. When that happens, you won't feel the pain of change because it is what you wanted.

Next time a change hurts you, think of one good thing that happened in your life because of change. Maybe you got more freedom to make decisions once you grew up, or lost touch with certain troublesome people. Change is of two types—one that hurts us, and another that we accept easily. If we can accept both equally, life becomes truly easy.

Social Media

Social media has led us to believe that happiness lies in a glamourous lifestyle. People have an easy way to highlight things they are proud of—their relationships, their vacations, or their looks. This gives them another way to design their public image which, in turn, feeds their ego.

The viewers of their content might not be interested in them, but they are likely to compare what they see with their own lives—wondering what's missing. They might overlook the fact that people only post about their joyous occasions—the day they got promoted, their surprise date, or their new house. They will not post videos of their fights with their partners, the long hours they worked before they got time off, or the heavy loan they were burdened with after buying a house.

Nobody's life has only achievements and no struggles; only happy relationships and no interpersonal issues. Social media platforms provide a distorted image of reality which sets unreasonably high expectations. Life is meant to be a party—a mountain with only peaks and no valleys.

While there is nothing wrong with people posting their happy moments or their achievements, it frequently leads to insecurity, jealousy, and a range of negative emotions. Besides comparison with others, people often use these platforms to stalk ex-lovers or keep tabs on *friends* whom they don't like, thereby increasing hostility and rivalry. A survey conducted on the consumers of social media content indicated that these platforms resulted in reduced self-esteem and depression.

If you have ever posted anything on social media, you might remember your excitement on receiving a response. Every time your post gets a *like* you experience a dopamine hit. You feel happy momentarily and soon you are waiting for more. This happiness is hard to sustain because there is no assurance of *likes*. Even if they do come in, it might not mean that we are actually *liked*. It gives us an illusion of having a relationship with lots of people because they happen to be around electronically. It doesn't provide us with one friend we can depend on amongst hundreds of them indicated on the platform.

To have a peaceful life, it helps to use these platforms in moderation. Periodically evaluate how they impact your emotions. Reflect—what is your objective of being on them? If you find nothing significantly useful, consider going off them for a short while. Gradually, extend the time. This is to increase your happiness by redirecting your time toward activities that uplift you.

If you enjoy being on social media, do so with moderation. Most platforms are designed to keep you on them for as long as possible. Their creators have given you the keys to a car that you can speed in but forgot to tell you how to get out of it. That's why you **endlessly** see posts as you scroll and why you are notified constantly for things that might not seem important at all. Awareness on how much time you are spending on these platforms and your objective of doing so is important for your well-being.

Consumerism

Consumerism is the idea that having more products and services is good for us. Our overall happiness depends on how well we collect these material possessions, regardless of whether we need them or not. This thinking serves the marketers well. They are happy to have more people on their sales graphs helping them meet their targets; the targets being us—the people.

We are made to believe that if we have a bigger house, a better car, or smarter outfits, we will make heads turn. The advertisements show people responding in awe to a person using their product. These incessant messages condition our thinking. They make us believe that having what they offer will complete us. If they allow us to be satisfied with the way we are, where will their products fit in?

When we have what we want in the amount we need, we are happy. Anything more than that leads to the stress of making decisions, additional expenses, and management. This is one reason why minimalism has gained popularity over the years. People realized that having less stuff made life simpler for them.

When we face excessive options, it creates the *paradox of choice*. We are confused which one to pick. Unconsciously, we fear making the wrong choice. American psychologist Barry Schwartz, in his book *"The Paradox Of Choice,"* said that reducing consumer choices reduces anxiety for shoppers. As he points out, there was a time when we had only one type of pizza and one type of jeans. If we wanted to buy one, we would walk into a store and ask for it. Today we have a dozen variations of each, making us wonder which one to pick. Considering hypothetical trade-offs burns up metabolic energy. We not only have to make a decision, but the *right* one!

Remember how you felt when you bought the latest version of a phone, only to see the price drop significantly soon after? Wanting *better* or *more* can set us up for these disappointments. When we don't have something, we feel like we are missing out and when we have it, we still fear a raw deal.

The concept of *more is better* has been sold to us by people who will benefit from it. They want us to believe that we are lucky to have plenty of choices. Building choices is good as it gives us more control over situations. As a coach, I create many choices for my clients so they get to select the best one for them. However, that needs to be done with discretion, otherwise our goals will be left in the side stands while our options race against each other in an endless quest for victory. Sometimes having less is more—fewer decisions, less expenditure, fewer things to manage, and overall less stress.

Unconscious Reprogramming

We are constantly bombarded with information, such as the things that are going wrong with the world or the glamour that is missing from our life. This programs our unconscious mind to focus on what's missing rather than be grateful for what we have. Once this becomes our usual way of thinking, feeling negative emotions is no longer a habit, it becomes expert behavior. We find it easier to enter those unhappy emotional states and stay in them.

We need to carefully choose the videos/movies we watch, the games we play, and the music we listen to, because every bit of information affects us. A study conducted on this subject concluded that children who play violent video games are more likely to demonstrate violent behavior in their lives. Similarly, people who are regularly exposed to good teachings are less likely to participate in criminal activities. This happens because the information we are exposed to impresses itself on our unconscious mind. After a point, we can't distinguish between imagination and reality; they seem the same.

Reprogramming our unconscious mind for happiness requires us to limit the time we spend doing things that pull us into negativity, such as incessantly checking our social media feed, talking negatively about others, or reading scary news articles. Instead, if we regularly listen to uplifting thoughts, read good quality material, and spend time with positive people, our mind gets filled with positivity. We become whatever we surround ourselves with. Choose what you have in your environment carefully—what you see, hear, and feel. This includes the people you engage with.

The Antidote to Ego

Each of us has a hunger for positive strokes. We like to feel loved and accepted. We also like to feel special. However, when this need exceeds a certain threshold, it results in grandiosity. People begin to feel they are a cut above others. They can't take *no* for an answer. They do things to others that they will not tolerate being done to them. There is no sense of equality.

Nobody wants to be around them. They can't understand why because they are oblivious to their faults. Their self-righteousness makes it difficult for others to have an intimate relationship with them. They are usually walking around with a patronizing, *holier-than-thou* attitude. Most of their relationships turn sour except with those who have accepted their superior status—even those few can't save them from their loneliness and disappointment.

I rarely meet someone who claims to have a big ego. It is usually something that others are able to notice in them. For those who are aware of it and want to work on it, there are a few things that can help. The antidote to a big ego is a dose of humility. Any kind of charitable work can do wonders in reducing an exaggerated sense of importance that a person might have.

When people volunteer at organizations that help the less fortunate, they tend to feel grateful for all that life has given them. Helping others releases a hormone in the body called serotonin. Acts of kindness and compassion promote this hormone which increases the happiness quotient of our mind and body. The interesting part about this is that we don't have to be the ones doing the act. Even watching an act of kindness can have the same effect on us. That's why we feel good when we see a young boy helping an old lady cross the street. When we watch the event, we experience the same release of chemicals as we would have if we were doing it ourselves.

We can experience the joy of giving by mentoring people who can benefit from our knowledge. This increases our knowledge as well as gives us the satisfaction of having contributed to the life of others. Another way to combat the egoistic voice is to learn from high performers and achievers. This is not to compare ourselves to others but to remind ourselves that learning is a lifelong process. Even the people who have achieved a lot know someone who has achieved more.

We all like to show our accomplishments to others or pin up our certificates on our walls. Appreciating and encouraging ourselves is a healthy thing to do. However, when it makes us feel like we are better than others and don't have more to learn, our growth ceases and we face unhappiness soon after.

12

———

SELF-ESTEEM

Our self-esteem is our subjective sense of worthiness. Since thinking is subject to distortions, we might not see ourselves for exactly who we are; our self-image could be larger or smaller than it is. We can't help but distort information as it is our coping mechanism to large amounts of incoming information. If the distortion is excessive, it could lead to feelings of inadequacy and stress. Let's go over the different levels of self-esteem and see how they could affect our happiness.

Low Self-esteem

Human beings need strokes to survive. A stroke is a unit of attention—anything that makes a person feel seen/heard/understood. The need for recognition is a powerful driver in human behavior. It makes us feel like we exist.

When people don't receive adequate strokes, they don't feel good about themselves. They compensate by self-aggrandizing or other-aggrandizing. Self-aggrandizing people have a sense of superiority over others, whereas other-aggrandizing people tend to feel inferior.

People with low self-esteem have an unequal status in relationships, which leads to unhappiness.

Self-aggrandizing

"I am better than you"

Egoistic people might seem powerful on the outside but suffer from low self-esteem on the inside. I remember being surprised the first time I heard this in my counseling class. It seemed counter-intuitive to me. Egoistic people don't think much of themselves? I imagined they thought too much of themselves. On further reflection I realized that an out-of-proportion self-image—be it much larger or smaller—falls in the category of low self-esteem.

As we saw in the section, Ego, a person who thinks of herself as above others has created an unhealthy self-image; one that will inadvertently be picked up by others. People are likely to respond negatively to such an image. When she sees that they don't like her, she will wonder what went wrong. Her outward portrayal of flawlessness will prevent her from expressing her self-doubt and clarifying things with them.

In moments of loneliness, she will feel sorry for herself and will think of ways she could get people to like her more. Unfortunately, none of these ways include treating others as equals. Her *larger-than-life* image takes a beating from time-to-time, eating away at her happiness. Her self-esteem remains low even though she appears to be proud of herself.

Due to the lack of authentic relationships, she is lonely. She can't share her genuine feelings with anyone. She wonders if people are talking about her behind her back. It is hard for her to trust them. She dislikes them for not being straightforward and blames them for not having a good relationship with her. She might not realize that *she* is a difficult person to have a good relationship with. People will not buy her grandiose facade and start liking her. Especially, since she subliminally gives them a message of her superiority.

Entitlement

Aren't they expected to abide by her because she is so much smarter? How can they treat her like this?

She feels entitled to be treated with respect, something she will not reciprocate. For instance, she might pick on other people for her entertainment but will not allow others to do the same. Due to her high expectations and sense of entitlement, people find it hard to connect with her. They can't tell her how they feel because they know she is not open to feedback.

They will grow closer to anyone with whom they can be vulnerable and talk about what hurts them—her behavior. Thus, the cycle of hurt and pain perpetuates. Gradually, people bond over a common problem (her!).

In the absence of authentic relationships, how does she satisfy her need for positive strokes? She tries to compensate by other means:

Shopping sprees: she stuffs her wardrobe with expensive brands and tries to improve her public image by peacocking. She might even become obsessed with her looks, believing that people would like her for them.

Addictions: she indulges in over-eating, drinking, smoking, drugs, or any substance that promises to create good feelings. This could also include promiscuous behavior, where she routinely enjoys physical intimacy with different people, intending to have fun and not develop any meaningful relationships. She could also indulge in activities that could numb her pain, such as playing video games, watching television, or surfing the internet.

Bragging: She works hard to polish her public image. If all goes well, people might buy into her grandiosity and start liking her too. She doesn't want to show her true self to others because she doesn't think highly of herself. She is scared that people won't like her if they got to know her. Maintaining two different images is tiring. Occasionally her mask drops, further stressing her out.

Controlling others: Since she has little control over herself, she opts to control others. It makes her feel powerful in the moment for which she pays later in the form of poor relationships.

A noteworthy quality in all the methods she could use to feel better is that they are **temporary**. One day the drug will wear off, the money will be spent, and the people she controlled will disappear, leaving her feeling emptier than before. She will have more to deal with after she has abused her body and frittered away her money. Her emotional problems will lead to physical problems as well as financial ones. It will be hard for her to stop this cascading effect, especially since she has no circle to support her.

Strength comes from deep and meaningful relationships. Instead of focusing on herself, if she focused on her relationships, she would experience more happiness. This was not possible for her because she never thought of investing time and effort into it. Sincere self-work can help her take responsibility for her life and turn it around.

Reflect-

Do you try to understand the perspective of others before expecting them to understand yours?

Do you indulge in any activities to numb your pain? Has it helped you? If not, what can you do instead?

Other-aggrandizing

"You are better than me"

A person who puts others up on a pedestal suffers from low self-esteem. She focuses on her weaknesses and the strengths of others. This comparison makes her feel inferior to others and reduces her self-esteem. If anyone tries to compliment her, she is likely to reject it because she feels unworthy of it. She blames herself for not being good enough and routinely brings it up in her conversations. She can't see anything nice in herself because she believes others aren't able to see it either. They get tired of her self-deprecating attitude and stop paying attention to her. This is how her loneliness begins.

She feels sorry for herself, believing that no one cares for her. She satisfies her need for strokes by blaming the people who are neglecting her. It is unlikely that someone will walk up to her and say, "Your consistent whining and nagging makes it impossible for us to be around you." Out of ignorance or compulsion, she continues her unrewarding behavior, until she has no one left to be with.

Another way she compensates is by people-pleasing. She believes that if she is very nice to others, they will be nice to her too. This might not be the case, as their behavior depends on their personality. Also, people-pleasers often put the needs of others ahead of their own. This might be a turnoff as people don't enjoy the company of a yes-man or a pushover. It is difficult to have an authentic relationship with someone who is just doing things to make them happy.

When they don't reciprocate positively to her efforts, she feels like a victim. Her poor self-image makes it even more difficult for her to stand up to the people she is angry with. She is likely to communicate her anger in a passive-aggressive manner because she feels unworthy of voicing her opinions. Either way, others will not work toward meeting her needs and will find it too complicated to be around her.

She might not realize that she is participating in what is happening with her. Clinging to people and doing all they want makes them lose respect for her. When they start taking her for granted, she believes *they* are at fault.

Reflect-

*Do you say **yes** when you want to say **no**?*

Do you believe you can get others to like you by being nice to them?

Do you consider your feelings to be as important as theirs? If not, how could you change that?

Both Roads Lead to Unhappiness

Low self-esteem is a common cause for unhappiness. It might not be an obvious one though because it is loaded with distractions such as anger, insecurity, jealousy, dominance, and blame games. Whether self-aggrandizing or other-aggrandizing, people suffer the consequences of their perceived unequal status with others. They develop unhealthy ways to meet their need for strokes, which results in poor relationships and subsequent unhappiness.

Healthy Self-esteem

We have gone over low self-esteem in detail. Let's look at the traits of people with a healthy self-esteem:

1. **Aware of their strengths/weaknesses**. They leverage their strengths and work on their weaknesses to achieve their goals. Their assessment of themselves is realistic. They are not scared to try out new things because they don't fear failure. (There is a thin line between confidence and overconfidence. When people become overconfident, their ego comes to the forefront, resulting in arrogance. It prevents them from enhancing their skills and giving their best.)

2. **Take good care of themselves.** They eat nutritious food, exercise, and relax when they need to. They don't abuse their bodies with excessive food, alcohol, drugs, etc. They dress well to make themselves feel good, not

to impress others. They don't worry about their appear-ances or people's opinions on it. Their strong self-image makes them naturally attractive.

3. **Have realistic expectations** of themselves and others. They don't believe they are entitled to anything. They don't have a long checklist of things people should do to make them happy. People don't feel burdened by their expectations and are free to be themselves.

4. **Don't compare themselves to others**. The only reason they might do this is to improve, not to put themselves down. Their worthiness comes from within and is not relative to the achievements of others.

5. **Take responsibility for their actions**. They are confident in what they do and don't feel the need to blame others when things go wrong. They own their mistakes and learn from them. This helps them stay in control of their life.

6. **Don't need praise/approval**. They are happy to be appreciated but they don't *need* it. They take praise and criticism alike. Hurtful remarks are treated as the person's view on them and not a measure of their self-worth. They don't people-please to gain approval.

7. **Don't cling**. They don't cling to people, things, or circumstances. This helps them adapt quickly to the changing scenarios in life. They do the same in their relationships as well. They don't cling to people, due to

which they are perceived as confident and attractive. People love a person who desires them without being needy.

8. **Believe all are equal**. They are assertive and can express their needs comfortably. They can say *no* to others and others can do the same, without any drama around it. They don't guilt and shame people into doing things. As a result, people find it easy to be around them.

9. **Stay authentic to themselves**. They practice personal integrity. They say what they think and mean what they say. They don't play mind games. People find it easy to trust them since they don't have to second-guess their views.

10. **Strong sense of purpose**. They follow their calling fearlessly. Their mind isn't clouded with self-doubt. If they want something, they go after it with the belief that they can have it. We will see this in detail in the section, Discover Your Purpose.

The Treatment Pattern

You can evaluate your self-esteem by reflecting on these three aspects of your behavior:

1. How do you treat yourself?

Check for Self-love:

When you make a mistake, how do you speak to yourself?

Do you feel good about yourself only when you have achieved something?

Do you celebrate the small victories in life? Or do you need something big to happen before you can be happy?

If you believe you are harsh on yourself, commit to being different going forward. Remember when you were a child, and you made a mistake, how it hurt you when adults rebuked you. Avoid doing the same to yourself. If you had someone whose soothing voice helped you feel better (or if you can imagine the type of person you would have liked to have back then) focus on the person's words and tonality. Use the same with yourself when you feel down.

Acknowledge that it's okay for things to go wrong from time-to-time—it happens to the best of us. Remind yourself of your achievements and appreciate yourself for getting so far. Talk to yourself like a kind friend would. That's the best gift you can give yourself.

Sometimes, people have difficulty appreciating themselves, especially when things aren't going well for them. The primary reason dates back to their early learning environment. In childhood, if a baby's parents complimented her only for *doing* things, she doesn't appreciate her *being* anything. For instance, if she told them that she spilled the milk and they punished her for it; they are responding to her *doing* something wrong, not the act of *being* honest. Similarly, if they praise her for coming first in class, she gets positive strokes for doing something, not for being the person who got there.

In such cases, the child will grow up to be a person who constantly needs to achieve things to feel worthwhile. *Doing* is important, her *being* is never enough; leaving her dissatisfied and hungry for more. If her parents didn't give her adequate strokes, it will lead to maladaptive patterns similar to the ones we saw in the section, Low Self-esteem.

If you feel like your small victories are not worth celebrating, check if you are minimizing your achievements or disqualifying the positive. It is important for your self-esteem that you appreciate all aspects of your life, big or small. Ensure you give yourself positive strokes for being who you are and not just what you do.

2. How do you treat others?

Check for Self-Aggrandizing Behavior:

When others make a mistake, how do you treat them? Do you try to understand their perspective and give them the benefit of the doubt?

Do you compliment people when you like something about them?

If you believe you are harsh with others or don't praise them enough, examine how you are with yourself. Your relationship with others is a reflection of your relationship with yourself. Any work you do on loving and accepting yourself more will improve your relationships with others as well. We will see this in the section, Steps to Develop Your Self-esteem.

3. How do you allow others to treat you?

Check for Other-Aggrandizing Behavior:

When hurt, are you able to stand up for yourself?

Are you able to communicate your feelings easily to others?

If you are not happy with the way others treat you, you need to communicate it to them. If you are unable to do so, go over what might be stopping you. Do you believe their feelings are more important than yours? Or do you find the thought of standing up to them scary?

When people don't treat us well and we do nothing about it, our self-esteem goes down.

The thought of not being able to protect yourself will lead to anxiety. If you can push back, even a little at a time, your confidence in yourself will build up, just like a muscle that strengthens due to regular exercising.

You cannot change how others think and feel about you. However, you can demonstrate how they should treat you by treating yourself well. Say *no* when you want to, so they understand that you respect yourself.

This will set the precedence for future interactions as well.

Steps to Develop Your Self-esteem

Your self-esteem impacts your feeling states, decisions, results, relationships—in short—your happiness. It's rare to find people suffering from low self-esteem and happy with their life. Going after things that matter needs courage to face uncertainty and risk failure that will be encountered on the journey. Without the ability to put oneself out there, it is impossible to achieve anything meaningful, be it good relationships or career aspirations.

People who love themselves have no reason to hide their true selves from the world.

Allow yourself to be seen. Your authenticity will be a welcome change to people who are tired of communicating with masks. If some people don't like you for it, it's okay for them to move on—better sooner than later. You will always find others who will appreciate you for who you are rather than what they want you to be. It is far easier to live this way because you have only one role to play—you.

As we saw earlier, poor relationships are linked to a person's level of self-esteem. We don't like people who have too big an ego (condescending, bragging, controlling) and we don't enjoy the company of those who look down upon themselves (self-pitying, complaining) either. We like people who are confident, assertive, and respectful, that is, with a healthy self-esteem. Here are some ways to develop it:

1. Don't dwell on negative experiences. We become like the people we think about. This happens because we vibrate at the frequency of our dominant thoughts and our biochemistry changes to adapt to it. Identify your distortions in thinking and challenge the ones that cause negativity. Practice ways mentioned in this book to gain closure and move past situations that hurt you.

2. Avoid comparing yourself to others unless it helps you learn or get inspired. If having the most or being the best at something could make a person happy, there would be only one happy person in every field (feeling anxious that he/she could be replaced any minute). The best comparison is with previous versions of yourself as it helps you measure your progress.

3. Set boundaries with others. Refrain from doing things just to make them happy. As long as you respectfully communicate your feelings, you are not responsible for how they take it. Avoid rescuing others from their feelings. It gives you a false sense of control because their feelings are eventually *their* responsibility.

4. Take responsibility for what happens to you. Blaming others when things go wrong could relieve you of the anxiety that comes with taking responsibility when

things go wrong. This could feel good momentarily but will also cause you to lose control of your outcomes.

5. Be kind to yourself. Taking responsibility for yourself doesn't imply blaming yourself. Engage in positive self-talk. You wouldn't want to live with a person who is constantly criticizing you. So, avoid doing it to yourself.

6. Do volunteer work. (Refer section: Antidote to Ego.)

7. Connect with your purpose. (More on this in the section: Discover Your Purpose.)

13

RELATIONSHIPS

The 80-year-old famous Harvard Study, conducted to find out what makes people happy, discovered something simple yet profound. They closely monitored the participants of their research program over decades—their trials, their victories, and setbacks—to understand what made them happy. One might believe it's material possessions, comfort, money, or fame. Interestingly, they found that the number one reason behind the happiness of their research participants was healthy relationships.

Our need to feel loved and connected is so deep that only when it is fulfilled can we enjoy other things in life.

People who had close relationships with their family members, friends, and communities, were overall happier than the ones who struggled with their relationships. Their bonds helped them stay centered when life rocked their boat, reducing their overall level of anxiety. Anxiety comes when you believe you are alone —up against the world without support. When you have people who care for you, love, and support you, the world seems easier to take on.

Investing time and effort in nurturing beautiful relationships leads to happiness.

Loneliness

Distortions in thinking lead to poor relationships, alienation, and stress. Loneliness is usually the result of a disproportionate self-image which causes people to cut themselves off from others. If they think they are better than others, that becomes a reason to not mingle with them; if they think they are worse, they won't have the confidence to approach them. Either way, they are alone.

Their distortions create walls around them that are hard to break. They stay captured in their forts, assuming that no one outside would like their company or that they should find better people to hang out with. Unfortunately, no one fits the bill.

What is strikingly common among most people who feel lonely is that they *think* no one cares for them. This usually isn't the case. The people in their lives could be busy or caught up with their own problems, due to which they aren't able to pay attention to them. Another person in their place might not feel as lonely. It is their perception that no one cares. Even if nobody does, they still have the option to go out and create new relationships. If they choose not to do so, it is their decision, not their condition that is stopping them.

Loneliness can make people anxious, angry, frustrated, and depressed. The best way out for people facing this is to stop thinking about how little others care and turn the focus inward on their distortions in thinking and self-esteem. Any progress made on these two fronts will make them more confident in initiating and sustaining healthy relationships.

(Refer sections: Distortions in Thinking and Steps to Develop Your Self-esteem. The methods presented in these sections will help shake deep-rooted unhelpful beliefs on one's self-worth and open doors to happier relationships, thereby eliminating loneliness.)

Expectations

You feel happy when things are the way you want them to be—your partner is perfect, your promotion is here, and your coffee is brewed. You can't think of anything else you would rather have. You are happy! It's only when things don't go your way that the test begins. Your ability to deal with unfavorable outcomes will now determine your level of happiness.

When your expectations are not met, you can be happy by expecting less or working toward getting them met. The best direction is contextual. Here are some pointers that can help you decide:

1) **Not in your control**: If your expectation relies on something that is not in your control, reframe the situation and let it go. For instance, if you wanted to go out with a friend who stood you up, you weren't responsible for what he/she did, but you are responsible for how you will manage yourself in the event.

If you want people to behave in a certain way for you to be happy, you will be dependent on a random event; one that will happen occasionally and unpredictably. Even a broken clock shows the right time twice a day, but it's not something that can be relied on.

Direct your efforts toward things you *can* influence, like your thoughts and feelings, rather than those of others. The idea of changing others can be an alluring one, but it rarely ever happens until we make some changes ourselves.

2) **Bears no result**: If your results repeatedly indicate that a certain expectation isn't getting you what you want, you might need to re-examine it. It would be nice if your relatives cared more, if your manager was less authoritative, or your friends kept in touch. However, despite communicating your needs, if you don't see a

change in what you receive, it might be time to let go of the expectation or the person.

According to Fritz Perls, the founder of Gestalt therapy, we are not in this world to satisfy the expectations of others, and others are not there to satisfy ours. If our expectations meet in the process of our interaction, it's good. Otherwise, there is only so much we can do about it. This does not mean to say that we allow people to walk over us. We have needs—to be seen, heard, valued, and respected. If we believe that somebody is being disrespectful toward us, we need to stand up for ourselves. The expectation of respect is not something that needs to be reduced.

On the other hand, there are expectations that can be worked upon. Let's say you want a loved one to care more for her health, believing it is good for her. You eat healthy food and exercise and you want her to do the same. If she doesn't, you get frustrated. It is the expectation that people should do as you want that creates the frustration, even though you had her best interest at heart. Unlike you, she might not see the need for it. Such expectations cause harm to the one who is holding them rather than benefit the one they are created for.

Perfection

The expectation of perfection pressurizes the one who is holding it as well as the ones who have to live up to it. While it is good to have high standards—as it is one way to improve constantly—it also helps to be mindful of the fact that people might not be able to do what you want them to. If we have an image inside our mind of how they *should be* and hold them up to it, we are setting ourselves up for disappointment because they might not measure up. (Refer section: Should Syndrome.)

If you are disappointed with someone not meeting your expectations, check-

Is what you are asking difficult for the person to do?

Could there be a reason why the person can't follow through with your request? If so, can you revise the expectation?

It is important to reflect on the expectation before allowing ourselves to feel disappointed in others. It also helps to listen intently to them when they are expressing their views. Their reason holds good for them even if we don't understand it.

I once knew a person who would expect his daughter to wake up at 6 am and jog. He said her stamina was poor and so she needed to exercise. Despite multiple attempts, the girl wasn't able to do what her father expected of her. Eventually, he got furious and gave up on her. A few days later, she was diagnosed with anemia. The deficiency of iron was making it difficult for her to run. When her father realized this, he experienced remorse.

Expecting more than people can give or are willing to give is like entering a game in which disappointment is assured. It helps to be happy with what we have, ask for what we can't do without, and act on what comes next. This might even mean that we walk away from certain relationships. It is essential to thoroughly examine the situation before doing so. Walking away hastily and frequently could result in loneliness.

Letting go

Letting go of a relationship isn't easy. The people we love live in our subconscious mind, and when they leave, they take that part of themselves with them. The longer our association with them, the more hurt we feel. Our mind plays back movies of our happy times, almost making us forget why we separated in the first place. Sometimes, we want to rewind time and bring them back into our life.

While separation in any relationship can leave a person disappointed, in my practice I have found that the self-esteem of youngsters is primarily affected by romantic relationships. When a romantic relationship falls apart people usually demonstrate signs of obsession and compulsion. When I'm on the phone and I hear a voice at the other end that is struggling to emerge, choked up with tears that the person is fighting back, it is usually a sign of a broken heart.

If the decision to move out of the relationship was

theirs, they often experience guilt. They consider themselves *bad* for having hurt someone's feelings. We work through this guilt by contemplating the future effects of continuing in a relationship that wasn't working out. After all, you can't be in a relationship only to keep people happy.

If they tried to make it work and drifted apart anyway, it is usually because the pain of being in the relationship exceeded the pleasure they got out of it. If they have underlying patterns of going from one relationship to another, then we evaluate which need of theirs is not getting met and how it can be met in a healthier manner.

Some common experiences of people who have had a broken relationship are that they:

1. can't seem to think about anything or anyone else.

2. wonder if the person remembers them.

3. don't believe they will find anyone else again.

4. replay old memories, wondering where they went wrong.

5. are, at times, tempted to call the person and patch up.

6. experience guilt at hurting the other person (if *they* called off the relationship).

7. imagine that there is something *wrong* with them and wonder why they can't find the right person.

8. are worried about what people will think about their break-up.

9. in extreme cases, don't want to live at all.

Their self-esteem is affected by this experience. It takes six months for most people and a little more for others, but things do get better with time. Here is what helps them come out of it faster:

1. Finding the support of friends, family, and professionals, such as a coach or therapist.

2. Allowing themselves to vent their emotions. Any deliberate attempt to stop thinking about the past reinforces feelings of despair and must be avoided.

3. Taking care of themselves. Walking, exercising, eating comfort food, and spending more time pursuing their hobbies.

If you feel like the loss of a relationship has caused you to become deeply unhappy, accept your emotions without trying to fight them. This is also a good time to bring the focus back to yourself. You might have already spent a lot of energy trying to make the relationship work. Now prioritize taking care of yourself. Spend time with people who make you happy and do the things you enjoy. Be assured that once you change

your state, the relationship you desire will find its way
to you.

14

DISCOVER YOUR PURPOSE

I have clients who have been working successfully for over 20 years in their respective organizations. Most have climbed up the ladder quickly and have even won awards for their performance. Despite this, they feel like something is missing. They have thoughts such as-

Where am I heading?

Why am I not happy with my achievements?

Is this all there is to life?

Overachievers might seem happy with their lives but they also suffer from existential questions, especially when they don't know the purpose of their life or cannot align with it. They sweep their questions under the carpet and get on with their busy lives, only to have them spring back another time.

Having a clearly defined purpose brings meaning to life. Fulfilling it brings happiness and satisfaction.

Find Your Passion

If you aren't sure of your life purpose, check with yourself-

What makes you happy?

What would you do if you were left alone for a day? (Assuming you have no access to television, video games, social media, and other devices that fragment your attention. Would you paint, write, play a musical instrument, or learn a new language?)

What did you enjoy doing as a child? Were you good at it?

What makes you lose track of time?

Was there any work you did in the past that didn't feel like work?

Achieving something difficult requires concentration for extended periods. When you are completely immersed in an activity, you achieve flow. It happens when the challenges you solve are meaningful to you. The word *meaningful* implies that the level of difficulty needs to be right for you—something just outside your comfort zone.

If I ask you to solve a second-grade math paper, you would find it too easy to be interested in. If I asked you to review the research paper of a scientist, and you are completely unaware of the subject, you might feel frustrated since you do not have the skills to complete such a task. Now think of a book that is appropriate for your level of knowledge and is aligned with your interests. If you were to read this book, you would immerse yourself in it and lose track of time. This flow is evidence of you doing what you like.

It can also be experienced when you follow your passion. Time flows and you find it easier to stay focused on a task for longer periods, thus producing excellent results. When you nurture your dream from something small to phenomenal, it boosts your confidence, self-esteem, and happiness.

Fragmented Attention

Distraction robs us of the flow that can be achieved through focus. We lose the ability to concentrate and remember things if we constantly switch between tasks. It also makes us impatient. We can't wait for the elevator to appear after we press the call button; we can't wait for our computers to boot up; we don't like to be behind people at a checkout counter. The increasing level of impatience is due to the constant distraction that fragments our attention—jumping between sites, playing video games, and checking our social media feed.

To generate optimum results, minimize your distractions by working in a place that has no access to social media, phone calls, emails, etc. Switch off all notifications. Instead of checking your messages and posts immediately as they appear, schedule them to a time of the day when you are usually not very productive. Avoid accessing anything that qualifies as a distraction until you have achieved a state of flow in your work.

Flow cannot be maintained beyond a certain period. If you concentrate well on a task, you will get tired after a while. Your mind might be lost in a state of flow but the body has a way of signaling its tiredness to you. For instance, you might change your posture—straighten your back, yawn, or stretch. This is a good time to take a break.

Talent

Wanting to do something and being good at it are two different things. While you can pick up any skill you want, having an aptitude for it will certainly be an advantage. Check with yourself-

Does your purpose align with your talent?

Every person in this world has a unique talent—something that comes easily to him/her as opposed to others. If you are aware of your talent, you can leverage it to do things that others find unimaginable. Here are a few ways to know where your talent lies:

1. Ask people who know you well what your core strengths are.

2. Get your work reviewed by experts in your field.

3. Enroll in a class. Evaluate your progress and discuss it with your trainers.

You might already know what you are good at, but you might not be the best judge of it. It always helps to get feedback from others around you. The more knowledgeable they are in your field, the better it is. This is an important step to avoid the frustration that might arise by signing up for something you like to do but are not cut out to.

Tread the feedback zone carefully. There will always be people who will discourage you from following your passion. They might not have achieved their personal goals, but are very sure of yours. You don't need to buy into their views. They will tell you that you aren't smart enough, you don't have the talent, you need more money, etc. They will serve you a dollop of their self-doubt (don't eat it).

Tap into the opinions of only those people who are knowledgeable in your field. If they have strived out of their comfort zone to achieve their goals, they are the ones to pay attention to. Spend time with your role models—people who have successfully achieved what you want. Request them to mentor you or volunteer to work with them. Their influence will help you pick up new skills and beliefs, which will motivate you to follow your chosen path.

Add Value to Others

What is the one thing that comes easily to you? What can others learn from you?

What value can you add to the life of others? How can their lives change because of your work?

When you care for something greater than yourself, it prevents you from experiencing self-pity or entitlement. This enhances your self-esteem and happiness.

You get what you want when you help others get what they want.

If you contribute to the lives of people you will always have a rich purpose in life. Ensure it is something you love doing. If you don't love what you do, you won't be able to add the value that is required.

Your Values

Imagine you are a soldier in an army that is about to embark on a battle. Your general explains the line of attack to you but you are unaware of the reason behind the war. What will you do? You will probably fight as directed because you were asked to. However, if you are told the reason behind killing the enemy is to protect your land, women, and children from being plundered, then how would you fight? With more vigor than before!

The battleground is your life; the enemy represents the problems that will crop up, and your purpose is what will keep you fighting. When what you do is in complete alignment with what is important to you, you need no motivation to do it. You will forgo pleasure and endure extreme pain because you value it.

We all have a hidden desire for a meaningful life, more than a happy one.

We often hear of people who risk their lives, trying to save others. They are not necessarily commandoes, doctors, or firefighters. They are regular people who aren't trained in rescuing others; they just acted based on their core value of caring. That's what people do— behave as per their values.

For you to act, your purpose needs to align with your values that are your powerful unconscious drivers.

Check with yourself-

What is important to you? If you get that, what will it get you?

What are you unwilling to compromise on?

(A list of values is available in my book, **Being Yourself Journal**. Download your free copy at romasharma.com)

If your values aren't clear, you will take them on from others and feel dissatisfied when things don't turn out the way you want them to. If you are unhappy with what you are doing currently, connect with your reason for doing it—why do you do what you do? If it is only for money or position and it doesn't serve any other purpose, delve deeper. Money, power, attention, and fame feeds the ego and keeps us distracted. It is okay to want them, but having them as a core objective causes frustration. No matter how much of these we get, we will always feel like we are missing something.

Situations change. What motivates you today might not motivate you tomorrow. Let's say a lady leaves her job to take care of her infant because that was important to her. As the child grows, she might feel the urge to get back to her job. She no longer thinks of taking care of her child as a priority; maybe because he/she has become more independent over time.

As you go through life, your priorities could change, making you wonder if the decisions you took earlier were wrong. One way to avoid this is to prioritize your values early on. Among your values, which are the most important ones? Align your goals with respect to them. For instance, if money is one of your criterion values, it doesn't help to do social work and feel dissatisfied over the negligible financial gain from it.

Money as Purpose

When people explore their purpose a common question that crops up is about sustenance-

Will it help me sustain my living? Will I be able to pay my bills?

They dream of monetizing their interests but don't dare to do so. The security of their present work is too comforting to risk.

We require money to live a good life. Our happiness depends on it. There is no joy in being in debt. However, excess money comes with its own issues—it needs to be managed, there is the fear of losing it, it attracts unwanted attention from others, etc.

Having a lot of money doesn't bring about happiness. If it could, we wouldn't see billionaires depressed. Setting high standards for our financial health is good but earning to feed one's ego isn't. Hence, it is important for us to know how much money we want and what need it will fulfill.

If your purpose is aligned with your values you will be motivated to monetize it. If it is aligned with your talents it will be easier to do so. It is incredibly fulfilling to make a living doing what you love. Regardless of your field, you will find people who have gained financial independence by walking on your chosen path. Analyze what worked for them and model what could apply to your life. Select a role model whose life situation closely matches yours. For instance, if you are a single parent with two kids who wants to make it as a graphic designer, it will be helpful to model another person who has achieved the same goal under the same ecological conditions.

People as Purpose

If your purpose is connected to certain people, they will become a part of your identity. If they were to distance themselves from you or you had to let go, it will cause sorrow and a sudden sense of purposelessness. For instance, if a lady's purpose is to raise her children, what will she do once they grow up? If a man's purpose is to financially support his wife, he will lose his purpose if she were to become financially independent. This is seen in romantic relationships as well. Some people make their entire life about one person. When that person breaks off with them, they lose their purpose.

Attachment to people is natural. However, it is equally important to nurture other aspects of yourself that you can enjoy, even without your loved ones. That way you are happy to be with them but don't *need* them to be happy. Neediness chases away people faster than anything else.

Develop a large circle of friends. This will spread your time and attention across a wider group of people. A small circle not only gives you less people to mingle with but also increases your expectations of the ones in it. If they are unable to cope with your expectations, they are likely to feel frustrated and distance themselves.

For instance, a girl who has only one friend expects him to go out for dinners, movies, games, and dancing with her. He might not be interested in *all* these things. He might like one or two, perhaps movies and dinner. If she has only one person to go out with the expectations on this person will be high. He is likely to feel pressurized and refuse to go out at all. If she had more friends she would have found people with varying interests. That way she would always have the company she is looking for. Even if one or two people parted ways for some reason, it wouldn't rock her boat.

When we make certain people the center of our life we tend to cling onto them. We do more for them and, in turn, expect them to meet all our needs. This *expectation* hurts our relationship with them although it elusively appears to be *them*.

Discipline

You are what you do repeatedly. When you have a purpose but don't act on it, you feel unhappy, because on the one hand you want to do something and on the other hand you aren't able to. This dissonance causes frustration.

Create mini-goals around your purpose and act on them regularly. If you want to become a photographer, click pictures daily; if you want to become a painter, paint every day. Whatever you want to become, find the action that will lead you to it and do it *every single day*. Consistent action will bring result to your intention.

Happiness gained from instant gratification is fleeting. When you spend time creating something that benefits the world and gives form to your purpose, your happiness lasts. You feel motivated to continue contributing.

Motivation is not only the cause of action, it is the result of it too.

Purpose is meaningless without self-discipline. Discipline is the fundamental mindset that keeps you in a routine and helps you make progress toward your goals. In the process, you will inevitably face challenges. Decide which challenges you would like to embrace even before you embark on your journey. Choose your battles before they choose you, otherwise, if your problems are thrust upon you, you will be unhappy.

Be relentless in your pursuit and show up every day despite the challenges that stand in your way. If you observe what works and are flexible to adapt, you will definitely succeed.

Relentlessness is the single most distinguishing quality of highly successful people.

(For a comprehensive guide on how to stay motivated while pursuing your biggest goals, please refer to my book, Thinking Habits for Definite Success.)

The Balance

If we have no purpose, it leads to existential frustration. People who are unhappy gnaw at others around them. They berate their children, criticize their partners, and are impatient with their co-workers. On the other hand, if they have a purpose and are attached to it they aren't happy either. Excessive desire to do something can prevent it from being fulfilled. Their obsession prevents them from enjoying what is in front of them—the present moment.

What we need is a balance between being attached to our purpose and not having one at all—a life where we do what we like to and enjoy the rewards mindfully.

What Stops You?

Very often I meet people who want to do something but are doing something else. This pull from both directions is damaging. They aren't happy with what they are doing and never get to what they want to do.

If you know your purpose but are scared to pursue it, check what is stopping you. Are you worried about failure or what people will think?

If you are scared it means you are going to do something really brave.

People who have a purpose are happier than those who live their lives based on whatever is expected of them. Be okay with not living up to everyone's expectations, being laughed at, or criticized. If you dare to stand out from the crowd, you will get some negativity come your way. Between people who criticize and people who act on their dreams, the action-takers will always be the happier ones, even if their dreams don't materialize. The fact that they tried boosts their self-esteem.

The people who put others down are unlikely to generate any results. They feel better about themselves when others fail. It gives them solace about not trying to find their purpose or following it. They might not realize that using other people's results to stay away from their own hurts their self-esteem more than going after them ever could.

There are also people who know their purpose but don't want to do anything about it, believing it's not required. They are earning well and leading a comfortable life. What's the need to add more work to this? It's interesting how having all these things can leave a person feeling unfulfilled.

If you have all you want and are unhappy, has what you have earned fulfilled its purpose? If not, go deeper into the *why* of what you do. Your purpose will have a clear *why*, even if you are unsure of the *how*. As long as you have a strong enough reason to do something you will find a way to do it. (Refer section: Your Values.)

When people are aware of their purpose but don't act on it, I usually ask them to reflect on how they would feel when they are old and they looked back at their life. Would they regret not having followed their calling? Would they wish they had lived more for themselves than others? Would they want another chance at life so they could do what they *always* wanted to?

The thought that we live only once is subliminally present in our awareness all along although it hits us only toward the end.

The best time to do what you want is now!

Next Steps

When you do what you love to do and it aligns with your talents, you will be successful at it. You will achieve flow and create phenomenal results. When others benefit from your work, you will experience the joy of contributing. A job well done boosts your confidence too. You reap the rewards in the form of money, name, fame, recognition, etc.

What next?

Don't allow these things to become objectives. They keep a person running after fleeting rewards. Your purpose is not one *goal* to be achieved but a *direction* to be followed; your values being the compass. It will give you a reason to wake up in the morning and gladly fight your battles.

15

WHAT'S MISSING?

Happiness is not an event that occurs, but a way of life. It comes naturally to us when the different areas of our life are in balance. Let's examine which of them are doing well and which ones need work.

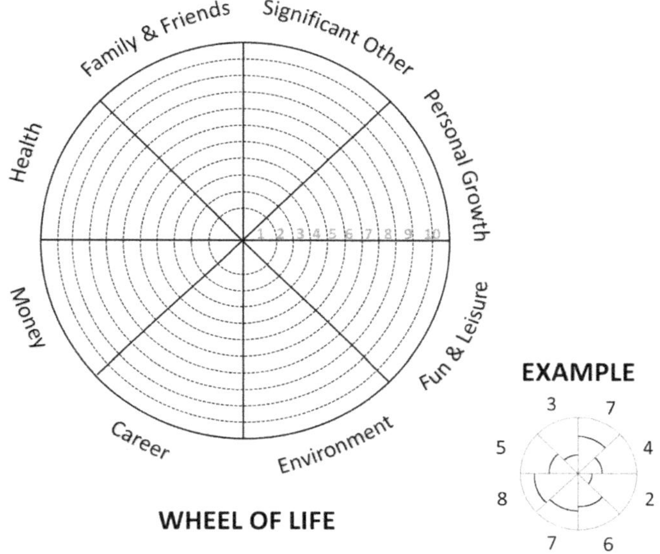

HEALTH: A happy mind resides in a healthy body. Take care of yourself by exercising regularly and eating moderately. Ensure you get your daily dose of sleep, food, and nutrition. Regular meditation, deep relaxation techniques, breathing exercises, and visualization techniques help in creating biochemical changes that support happiness.

Career: Does your career make you happy? Does it fulfill your needs, financially and psychologically? If it doesn't, contemplate your purpose and create a plan around it that could lead to your satisfaction. (Refer section: Discover Your Purpose.)

Money: We need money to fulfill our necessities, without which we would be anxious and insecure.

Check with yourself—do you feel financially secure? If not, what would financial security look like and how can you attain it?

Friends & Family: As human beings, we have emotional needs that can be fulfilled by connecting with people who love us and appreciate us. The feeling of belonging to a group makes us feel secure—something we can't get from other sources. Invest in relationships with people who encourage you to live up to your greatest potential. Disassociate from toxic people. Even when you do so, avoid carrying negative thoughts about them. (Refer sections: Relationships and Dealing with Bad Memories.)

Significant Other: If you have a significant other, how is your relationship with him/her? How can it be improved?

Studies have shown that having difficulty in the primary relationship can lead to persistent sorrow. This could be because of the degree of engagement we have with our partners as opposed to others. More interaction provides more opportunity for differences, and when that happens it becomes difficult to get some space from the person we are closely associated with. Our emotional entanglement prevents us from gaining clarity on our situation.

One way to have a pleasant relationship with your significant other is to select a person with whom your values match. You can adjust in a troublesome relationship with mismatched values too, but this will take up a lot more energy than you might be willing to spare.

Personal Growth: Are you living the kind of life you want? Would you say you are evolving as a person? Prioritize your personal growth by making goals around self-improvement. Keep yourself accountable for achieving them. Make your thinking more effective by journaling your thoughts and challenging your distortions regularly. Nurture your inner child by practicing self-love. Look at yourself in the mirror every day and say one thing you like about yourself. Work toward building your self-esteem; it will open more doors to happiness in the form of good relationships. (Refer section: Steps to Develop Your Self-esteem.)

Fun & Leisure: What do you do for fun? Do you make time for it in your life? Include activities in your daily routine that you enjoy, such as listening to music, playing sports, or reading. Spend time every day cultivating your hobbies. This will release happy hormones in your body and give your day a mood-lift. Getting a massage is a good way to de-stress. It stimulates your inner child and releases oxytocin, which helps you stay calm.

Physical Environment: Have you gone to a place and felt good instantly? Your physical environment has a direct impact on your mood. Your office and home are where you spend most of your time. Having a well-maintained place that supports your needs while you work or rest is essential to your well-being. Check with yourself—do you like your workplace and your home? Is your workplace conducive to productivity? Is your house comfortable?

The eight sections of the wheel are discussed separately but aren't disjointed. An improvement in one improves others as well.

Here are a few examples:

Case 1: A person is financially secure but is unhappy because she doesn't have a significant other in her life. She has a good physical environment and sufficient money but she doesn't make time for fun and leisure. If she goes out and has fun it might also help her find the partner she is looking for.

Case 2: A person doesn't have a job. Her financial insecurity leads to a poor relationship with her significant other. She doesn't have the money to go out with her friends and have fun either. If she gets a job, many areas of her life will improve simultaneously.

Case 3: A person works hard at her job and is financially secure. However, she doesn't make the time to nurture her relationships. She likes to play basketball but doesn't find the right company for it. As a result, she doesn't play either. She becomes a workaholic because it serves as an easy distraction from her loneliness. Her health deteriorates. If she schedules some time toward building her relationships she might find someone to play basketball with too. This will promote her physical fitness and reduce her loneliness, thereby improving her health.

The different areas of your life need to synergize for you to be happy. They are not watertight compartments. Whatever impacts one, impacts others as well.

Exercise

1) Draw the Wheel of Life on paper. Mark and label the eight sections.

2) What would a satisfying life look like in each section? Rank your level of satisfaction with each area of your life by drawing a curved line across the corresponding segment. Imagine the center of the wheel is zero and the outer edge is 10. Score between 1 (very dissatisfied) and 10 (fully satisfied). Refer to the **Example** wheel in the Wheel of Life Diagram.

3) Create a new outer edge for the wheel. The new perimeter represents the wheel of your life.

4) Identify at least one action item to improve your score in each section of the wheel and improve your life balance.

If this were a real wheel, how bumpy would the ride be?

16

AFTERWORD

Disappointment requires programming. You already know what will make you unhappy from your experiences so far. What if you could decide to not let those situations bother you in the future? What if you could program yourself to become calmer as things get difficult? You are the only thinker in your universe, and if you decide to reprogram yourself, nobody can stop you.

Plan for wonderful feelings by imagining positive things in the future. Whatever you want, just believe you can have it, even if you don't have a good reason to think so at the moment. Your conviction will draw situations and circumstances into your life that will manifest what you desire.

Sometimes your happiness might stray away due to what others said or did. You might lose energy trying to change things that are not in your control, like what other people think and feel about you. Bring your focus back to *your* thoughts and feelings. It helps to work on what you can control rather than try to fix problems that aren't yours to begin with.

If you think excessively about others, you will lose energy. The same happens when you think a lot about yourself. Your mind wanders into the past—how you were treated, how people didn't support you, how they blamed you, etc.—or into the future where uncertainty clouds you. As you continue to think about yourself, you will feel tired doing absolutely nothing else.

Overthinking is the invisible door to unhappiness because you pass through it unconsciously. Practice being aware of your feelings so that when you get absorbed in an overthinking trance you can switch tracks. The best way to switch is to create thoughts of adding value to others—what can you do to improve their lives? How can you leave a positive impact on this world? These thoughts will connect you to your higher purpose and remove the temporary discomfort you might face in the present moment. When you are giving something to someone it is the only time you are outside yourself. Your problems don't exist in that frame of mind.

Caring for others does not mean giving up on what you want. Happiness lies in the balance of things—doing what you like and what helps others as well. If you care more for what you want, you can't experience the happiness that comes from giving, and if you care more for others, you will feel like you are living a compromised life. Strike a balance between giving and taking, because neither is fulfilling by itself; just like to live, you need to breathe in and out in balance.

Treating people with kindness improves your self-esteem. It starts with treating yourself well. In my sessions, I have often noticed that when people are stressed, they become hard on themselves; expecting themselves to chin up and face their challenges, to impress people, or achieve more. When they tell me the expectations they have of themselves, I feel pressurized just listening to them.

When the going gets tough, the tough gets going is a saying that encourages people to do what they can't do or don't want to, increasing their difficulties. Be gentle with yourself during challenging times. Being *tough* and getting what you want will not be fulfilling unless you love yourself unconditionally.

Each one of us has a hidden desire to live up to our greatest potential. We may seek self-actualization in money, becoming wonderful parents, doing great academically, or by expressing our creativity. We seek recognition and love to feel special. The easiest way to ensure a constant supply of this feeling is to give it to yourself. Acknowledge everything you have overcome to be where you are today. Appreciate yourself for what you *are* and not just what you achieve.

Happy people don't necessarily have the best of everything. Their perspective on what they have helps them feel that way. They are in a habit of interpreting situations positively. What seems like a *problem* to others might not seem like one to them.

Our happiness doesn't lie in what happens to us but in the meaning we give to what happens.

Happiness may be our favorite emotion, but is hardly something that helps us lead a good life by itself. Anger, sadness, and fear are helpful emotions in making excellent choices. Without these, we will not know what is right for us and what isn't; when to pursue something, and when to run. Our survival depends on these emotions.

Fulfilling our needs makes us secure; growth makes us happy; wanting much more than that can be stressful, like striving to find water in a mirage that appears in another place as soon as we arrive. We want to live each moment to the fullest rather than chase illusions in the horizon.

While reading this book, you might have found some sections more applicable to you than others. Return to those sections, do the exercises present in them, and reflect on what you've found.

Knowledge isn't helpful without action.

The best way to counter unhappiness is with determination. Once you discover the area that needs work, create an action plan to improve it. Design mini-goals around the changes you want to see in your life and actively work toward achieving them.

If you already know what you need to do to be happy but aren't willing to do it, there might be a story you are telling yourself as to why you can't—maybe you are tired, you think it's too hard, or someone told you that you can't. Regardless of the reason, change is yours the moment you claim it.

Start today by rewriting your story and making it like how you would like to tell it tomorrow.

To Your Happiness,

Roma

Please Review This Book

We have reached the end of the book and I sincerely hope that you have found the answers to what will make you happy. I have a request for you. If you liked the book, would you please let others know about it?

1. Please leave a review on an online store that is convenient for you. (If you log onto romasharma.com and click on the book, you will find the list of storefronts where it is available.)

2. Share it on Facebook, Twitter, Instagram, Pinterest, or LinkedIn.

3. Please mention it to your circle of family, friends, or colleagues.

Reviews help readers discover books they like. They are the best way to get the word out. Even a line or two of your views on the book will help.

Thank you for taking the time to do this. Your support is much appreciated. I look forward to reading your views.

WHAT WILL PEOPLE THINK? (BOOK PREVIEW)

Here is a preview of the Book, **What Will People Think?**: How to be Confident in Yourself and Stop Worrying about What People Think. **Book 1 of the series.**

Why is What People Think Important?

We live in an ecosystem which entails give and take in our relationships. That's the only way for us to survive. It's important to us that other people like us. Life just becomes easier that way. We don't have to live in the uncertainty of *'Do they like me?'* or *'Don't they like me?'*. We just know and we can get on with our lives. When we do things that other people don't approve of, the contention saps us of our energy. Getting people to understand our perspective or to accept it can be quite exhausting. When we don't want to spend that kind of energy, we try to play it safe by just doing what they think is right.

The Reptilian Brain

Conforming to the group's expectation is a primal instinct. It comes from the two-million-year-old brain in us called the *reptilian brain*. If an animal was left out of the group, it could end up being eaten up by other animals or could fall prey to some other calamity. To ensure the survival of their species, animals developed what is known as the *herd mentality* according to which *staying together* was a way of *surviving together*. This is applicable even today. Our reptilian brain considers the opinions of people around us to be important. As a result, we might do things we never really wanted to do, in order to gain approval from others, in turn, sacrificing ourselves. That way, we sign up for short-term gain and long-term loss.

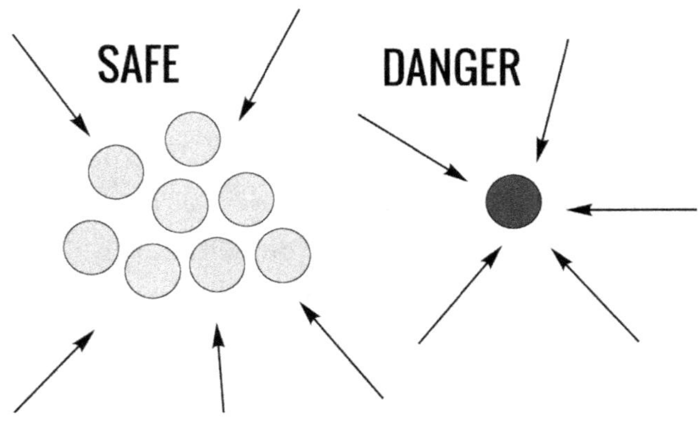

Staying together feels safe to the Reptilian Brain

We can see how advertising and marketing leverage on this point to sell to us. They show a person flaunting beautiful hair or driving an amazing car that makes heads turn in admiration. When onlookers are in awe of this person it makes us believe that their product will help us have a great public image too (one that they know is important to us!).

Approval Seeking as a Child

Sometimes the need to satisfy others could be really strong. This happens particularly if, during childhood, the parents were too strict, over-reacted when the baby made mistakes or had high expectations. A baby doesn't have a way to survive but to hope that her parents love and accept her, in the absence of which, she could feel really threatened. Her fear makes her feel like she is constantly walking on eggshells. She could become extremely adaptive and start doing things her parents want just so that she wouldn't displease them. This becomes a way of life, so she rarely thinks about what she needs. The focus is on pleasing the parents because that's the safest thing to do.

Rejection feels like death to an infant. When the baby grows into an adult, this child state continues to be in her. The approval of parents or primary caregivers is important, failing to receive which she could go through life seeking it in others and feeling the pain of rejection every time she doesn't get it.

The difficult parent is no longer around but is replaced by other people. These people have different faces but similar traits. She now tries to gain their approval in her life and continues to feel anxious when it comes to confronting them in any way. It makes her increasingly remorseful as her needs are not being met. She does not want to attract people who are like her difficult parents but that's what she unconsciously does because that is familiar to her and whatever is familiar feels safe.

It's important to note that the approval of *everyone* is not equally important to us. There is different weightage given to the approval of different people in our lives based on where we have placed them in our self-defined hierarchy.

Identity Decides Weightage

When it comes to people we look up to it is difficult for us to ignore their opinions. These could be people who care for us deeply or were there for us through thick and thin. We love them so much that we can not see them hurt in any way. Their opinions are as important to us as our own, maybe more.

When we care for a person's opinion it implies that he/she has a certain identity in our world. The more we regard this person the higher is the value placed on his/her perception. For instance, you might have been praised by a subordinate and it felt good. However, an appreciative comment from a person you look up to in your supervisor's circle might have meant more.

Identity decides the weightage given to an opinion. The greater the identity, the more the weightage.

This also implies that if you create an identity for yourself in somebody's world, your opinions will gain more credibility. You will be in a position to influence that person easily.

When there is conflict with people who mean a lot to us, we might end up doing things only to make them happy. In this case, we need to remember that the responsibility for what we are doing is ours, not theirs! The moment we shift the responsibility onto them we lose power and enter the dreaded game of hurt, pain, disappointment and shame.

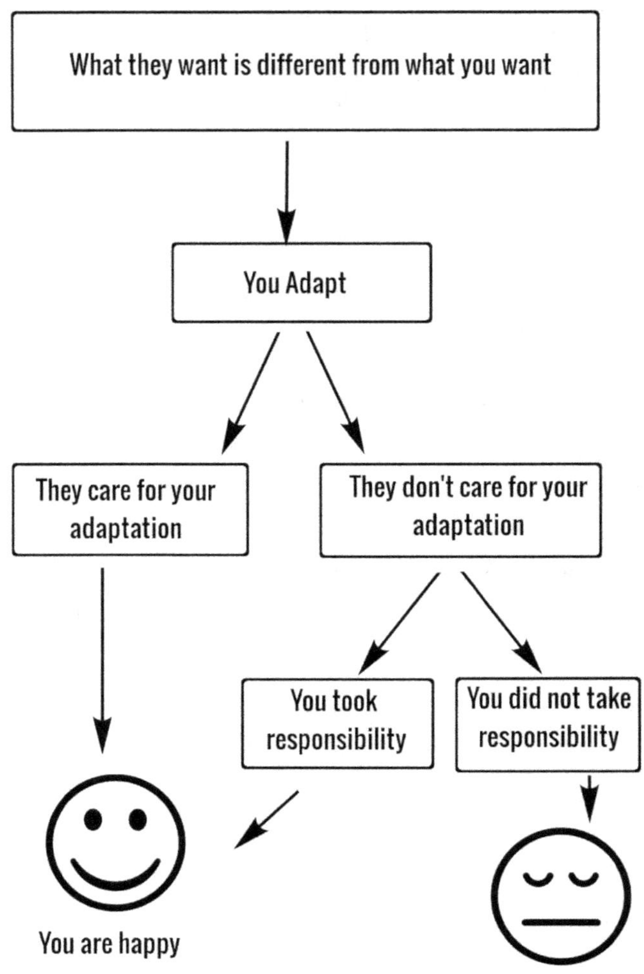

When we are caught in the middle of conflicting opinions, it helps to hash things out and find a middle ground. This can be done by asking others for what we need and at the same time being mindful of their needs. If the needs of any one side become more important than the other, it creates an imbalance in the relationship. If we are always adapting to what they want, we feel mistreated. If they are always adapting to what we want, they feel mistreated. A balance between the two sides brings stability to the relationship.

Being considerate about what people want is not the same as trying to please them. It's not possible for people to *become* happy with us without their mental participation in it. So, if we are more invested in the relationship than the other person is, it doesn't assure that the person will return our love and affection. In a relationship, we need both people to participate. One person can not decide to run the relationship. Hence, the expectations from our adjustments will need to be set as such. It helps to find a way that is mutually beneficial and take responsibility for what happens next.

Being Confident in Yourself

Adapting beyond a certain point to others creates a perception of you which could result in more expectations of adjustment coming your way. Hence, adapting needs to be done in moderation while continuously observing the results of doing so. When you don't worry about what people think, you reclaim your power and become attractive to those who desire this quality.

People like people who are like them or like someone they want to be. If I am anxious and I meet a relaxed person, it's natural for me to like that person. I might also wonder what makes him/her so easy going because I want that quality at some level. We don't pursue people as much as we pursue the energy they emit—something that they have and we want. People who like themselves and are not caught up in others perceptions of them can be great to be around. That's how we can create an amazing image of ourselves—by not trying too hard to do it! Counter-intuitive, isn't it?

When you don't try to control others and achieve what you want anyway, your confidence goes up through the roof. You feel it and others feel it too!

There are many merits to having a great public image. It helps us coexist with others in our ecosystems, gets us promotions and perks at our workplace and invitations to connect with more people socially. However, the problems begin when this image that is being created becomes very different from who we really are and unfortunately more important too. It's tiring as a lot of energy is spent in holding up that self-created image.

There are easier ways to create a good image on auto-pilot. For instance, we can demonstrate qualities of care and understanding towards others, which will help us create a good image without trying to do so. Care needs to be taken to ensure that we develop these qualities genuinely at a personality level and not superficially, intending to get something from others. If that is the case, people will sense it sooner or later. The relationship that could have been developed as a result of our good image will not stand a chance and the behavior to understand others will be viewed with skepticism.

So how can we confidently be ourselves, not worry about others and at the same time effortlessly create a great image? We are going to deal with every aspect of this in the upcoming sections. Let's start with understanding how we create our interpreted reality and what we can do to modify it in our favor.

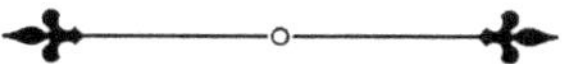

Did you enjoy the preview of the book?

Log onto romasharma.com and buy your copy of *What Will People Think?* **today!**

In the book, **Thinking Habits For Definite Success**, you will find a step-by-step guide to develop a success mindset that can transform your career, health, and relationships.

What readers say about the book:

"Inspirational examples explained logically"

"Recommended to anyone looking for a life-changing experience"

Log onto romasharma.com and buy your copy of *Thinking Habits For Definite Success* today!

ABOUT THE AUTHOR

Roma Sharma is a Certified Coach and Trainer who has been working in the field of emotional well-being since 2014. She runs a training company that authors programs for people from a variety of backgrounds—IT Industry, Educational Institutions, Counseling Academies, and Hospitality Industry to name a few. She works with organizations to design programs that specifically address their training needs.

Roma has a keen interest in understanding human behavior and connecting with people at a deeper level. Besides training and coaching, she regularly hosts a meetup in her city to discuss various topics related to mental health.

She likes to take up issues that her audience members experience in their day-to-day life and provide them with clarity so that they can devise simple solutions that consistently work for them. She has had the privilege of watching her clients become very successful in attaining the transformation that they set out to achieve.

When she is not training, she loves to bake cakes, read books, and play with cats.

Credentials:

- B.E (CSE)
- Diploma in Counselling Skills, person-centered therapy
- International Certification in Transactional Analysis 101
- Foundation course in Transactional Analysis
- Master practitioner of NLP (ABNLP), NLP Trainer
- Advanced Diploma in Hypnosis (Business-NLP, UK)

STAY IN TOUCH

Here are the best ways to stay in touch with me:

Subscribe to my Newsletter

Please leave your mail ID at **romasharma.com/newsletter** to receive articles on the best coaching practices, free video training programs, and eBooks.

Like my Facebook Page

Hit the like button on my Author Page **facebook.com/romasharmawriter** to receive the latest news from the world of coaching and the best offers on my new releases.

DOWNLOAD YOUR FREE 'BEING YOURSELF JOURNAL'

I hope you have downloaded your copy of the journal. If you have not, here it is again.

The Being Yourself Journal with powerful self-coaching questions is available at romasharma.com

Here is what you will find in the journal:

1. Page templates you can fill out every day to connect with your thoughts and feelings
2. Affirmations to increase self-esteem and confidence
3. Self-coaching questions that will help you find solutions in difficult situations
4. Simple ways to decrease worry and stay calm in the present moment

Journaling is a powerful way to understand yourself better. The way you feel about your thoughts changes when you write them down. If you journal on a regular basis you will find that—in a matter of time—your journal will become the single most useful document you have on yourself.

Whether you need to find a solution to a problem or just vent out your feelings, your journal is available to you whenever you need it. Download your copy and start journaling today.

Download now! Log onto romasharma.com

www.ingramcontent.com/pod-product-compliance
Lightning Source LLC
LaVergne TN
LVHW051258200726
843510LV00010B/1177